VARIATIONS

SIMPLE AND DELICIOUS DISHES. TWO WAYS.

By the author of The Silver Platter cookbooks
Daniella Silver

Photography by Jasmine DeBoer
Food Stylist & Culinary Producer by Abe Wornovitzky
Art Direction by Atara Yunger

Published by **ARTSCROLL / SHAAR PRESS**
4401 Second Avenue / Brooklyn, NY 11232 (718)
921-9000 / www.artscroll.com

Distributed in Israel by **SIFRIATI / A. GITLER**
Moshav Magshimim / Israel

Distributed in Europe by **LEHMANNS**
Unit E / Viking Business Park / Rolling Mill Road
Jarrow, Tyne and Wear / NE32 3DP / England

Distributed in Australia and New Zealand by
GOLDS WORLD OF JUDAICA
3-13 William Street / Balaclava, Melbourne 3183
Victoria / Australia

Distributed in South Africa by **KOLLEL BOOKSHOP**
Northfield Centre / 17 Northfield Avenue Glenhazel
2192 / Johannesburg, South Africa

ISBN-10:1-4226-2333-5 / ISBN-13: 978-1-4226-2333-6

Printed in Canada

ACKNOWLEDGMENTS

To my husband, JEFFERY SILVER, who has supported me throughout another cookbook. Your excitement, testing, and encouragement are everything to me.

To EMILY SILVER — thank you so much for helping me come up with a title for the book. You are so amazing and I love you so much.

To ALISHA SILVER, for always caring and asking how my shoots were every day after school. Thanks for testing the food; I love you so much.

To SORELLE SILVER, for having such a sharp eye. You are only 7, but I trust your attention to detail. I love you so much.

To ABIE SILVER, for joining us during our shoots when you got out of school at 2:30. I love you so much, my handsome!

To my mom and partner, RESA LITWACK, for literally being there for me every step of the way. You guided me throughout and your opinion means the world to me. I loved all the time we spent together! Thanks, ALAN, for being such a great support and a fantastic taster.

To my sister, ATARA YUNGER, whose talent doesn't stop. Once again, this book shines and it's because of your beautiful vision. Even though you are so far away, I feel so close to you. Thank you so much for turning my cookbooks into reality.

To my grandparents, NOREEN AND CYRIL LAX, for being the best editors and passing down the artistic genes.

To my mother-in-law, BONNY SILVER, for your constant love and support and for inspiring me to always cook from scratch. I know how proud you are of me.

To my dad, ARIEH GLUSTEIN, for being a huge help by proofreading and testing each and every recipe. All your compliments were so encouraging. Thanks also for stepping up and helping me with the editing process.

To my siblings, nieces, and nephews — ATARA, GADI, NERIYAH, ITAI, and SINAI YUNGER; ZVI, NAOMI, ILAN, SARI, and LIOR GLUSTEIN; SHERRI AND HANANEL SEGAL; JEREMY, TALYA, and LAYLA SILVER. You all are constantly supporting me, and I love you all so much! Thanks for being the best family!

To ABE WORNOVITSKY — What can I say — third book and we did it again! I'm so proud of the products we produced together. You are extremely talented, and it was such a pleasure to work with you again.

To JASMINE DEBOER — You are so talented, and it was a pleasure working with you.

SHARONA ABRAMOVITCH, RD MSC — Thank you for all your help with the nutritional analysis.

To ALTHEA CASTILLO and MARILAC RIVERA, my sous chefs in the kitchen. You both allowed me to work by keeping things calm in the house; thank you.

GEDALIAH ZLOTOWITZ, for supporting me. Having ArtScroll behind my cookbooks a third time is an honor. Thank you for your constant guidance and support.

To the ArtScroll team — FELICE EISNER, DEVORAH COHEN, TOVA OVITS, and JUDI DICK — thanks for all your help once again. It's so nice to work with you both so comfortably after all these years, with the relationships we've built.

NORENE GILLETZ — my mentor. Not much more to say than thank you for teaching me everything I know. You are one of a kind — a brilliant woman — and I feel so honored to have the relationship and closeness we have.

To my amazing supportive friends — for testing, helping, stopping by, editing, and so much more ... you guys mean so much to me — CHAYALA BISTRICER, DANIELLA GREENSPAN, STEPHANIE GREENWALD, EMILY HERSHTAL, PAMELA KUHL, SHOSHANA SCHACHTER, CHANTAL ULMER, and DORI WEISS.

CONTENTS

Acknowledgments 3

Introduction 8

APPETIZERS

Corned Beef Topped Eggplant 14

   Individual Eggplant Rounds 15

Turkey-Wrapped Enoki Mushrooms ... 16

   Turkey Wraps on Salad 17

Sesame Seed Rice Balls 18

   Fried Rice Balls 19

Deli-Wrapped Squash Bites 20

   Squash Bites on Spoons 21

Crunchy Chicken Kale Salad 22

   Chicken Kale Wraps 23

Deli Egg Rolls 24

   Deli Rice Paper Rolls 25

Corned Beef Biscotti 26

   Beef-Wrapped Biscotti 27

Cucumber Roll Ups 28

   Cucumber Boats 29

Zaatar Avocado 30

   Avocado Slices / Guacamole 31

Cute Baguette Cups 32

   Bread Cup Ideas 33

Lemon Herbed Bone Marrow 34

   Bone Marrow Spread 35

Dill Pickle Football Wings 36

   Pickle Chicken Bites 37

SOUPS

Healing Celery Soup 40

   Refreshing Celery Soup 41

Sweet Potato Pear Soup 42

   Cinnamon Sugar Pears 43

Toasted Garlic Panko Topping 44

Crunchy Seed Topping 44

Spiced Popcorn Topping 45

Chunky Mushroom Soup 46

   Pureed Mushroom Soup 47

Spiralized Noodle Soup 48

   Zoodle Chicken Soup 49

Healthy Tomato Lentil Soup 50

   Mason Jar Lentil Soup 51

Vegetarian Vegetable Quinoa Soup 52

   Shredded Vegetable Soup 53

Broccoli Soup With Caramelized Leeks ... 54

   Cauliflower Soup

   With Caramelized Leeks 55

Roasted Kabocha Squash Soup 56

   Soup Bread Bowls 57

Dinner Steak Soup 58

   Tofu Soup 59

SALADS

Simply Sweet Mini Pepper Salad 62

   Peppers 'n Dip 63

Pea Shoot Salad 64

   Mason Jar Salad 65

Fresh Herb Granola Salad 66

   Endive Boat Salad 67

Avocado Lentil Salad 68

   Avocado Bowls 69

Panko-Topped Kale Salad 70

   Kale Rice Rolls 71

Black And White Avocado Salad 72

   Avocado Lettuce Cups 73

Shredded Kale and

Brussels Sprouts Salad 74

   Teacup Salad 75

Baby Romaine Halves

With Lemon Dressing 76

   BBQ Romaine Salad 77

Pretty Brussels Sprouts Salad 78

   Quinoa Brussels Sprouts Salad 79

Rainbow Bright Salad 80

   Rainbow Salad Bowls 81

Baked Mini Falafel Ball Salad   82
    Kale Falafels   83
Three-Toned Cabbage Salad   84
    Individual Colored Salad   85
Hemp Heart Cucumber Salad   86
    Hemp Cucumber Cups   87
High-Fiber Salad Topper   88
    Fiber Topper/Snack   89

FISH

Hawaiian Poke Bowl   92
    Baked Salmon/Tuna Bowl   93
Honey Mustard Pretzel Bites   94
    Pretzel Salmon   95
French Fried Onion Salmon   96
    Salmon Bagels   97
Lemon Herbed Salmon Rolls With Asparagus   98
    Salmon "Sushi"   99
Pretty Pomegranate Salmon   100
    Fig Salmon   101
"Smashed" Salmon   102
    Salmon Salad   103
Black Sesame-Crusted Fish   104
    Fish Tacos   105
Salmon With 3 Spice Rubs   106
    Spiced Rubs   107
No-Mayo Avocado Tuna Salad   108
    Tuna Nachos   109
Crispy "Popcorn" Fish Bites   110
    Fried Fish Fillets   111
Lemon Dill Fish   112
    Pepper Dill Fish   113
Seared Sriracha Honey Salmon   114
    Topped Sriracha Salmon   115

CHICKEN

Sweet Granola Chicken   118
    Granola Chicken Tenders   119
Sheet Pan Chicken With
Heirloom Carrots And Sweet Potatoes   120
    Shredded Chicken Bowl   121
Kale Chicken   122
    Kale-Stuffed Chicken   123
Old-Fashioned Bbq Chicken   124
    BBQ Drumsticks   125
Lemon Rosemary Chicken   126
    BBQ Chicken Skewers   127
Salami Hasselback Chicken   128
    Salami Chicken Bites   129
Rustic Sheet Pan Chicken   130
    Rustic Couscous   131
Glazed Grilled Chicken   132
    Grilled Chicken Skewers   133
Tomato Garlic Chicken   134
    Tomato Chicken Topper   135
Baked Almond Flour Chicken   136
    Almond Flour Schnitzel   137
Honey-Glazed Sunflower Seed Chicken   138
    Pumpkin Seed Chicken   139
Spaghetti Squash Chicken   140
    Chicken In Squash Halves   141
Potato Latke Schnitzel   142
    Sweet Potato Schnitzel   143
Honey Mustard Chicken and Steak Dinner   144
    Rice Noodle Dinner   145

MEAT

Skirt Steak Strips With Tahini Herb Sauce   148
    Skirt Steak Tahini Salad   149
Sesame-Crusted London Broil   150
    Steak Bites   151
Bruschetta London Broil   152
    London Broil Crostini   153
Marinated Hot Pepper Brisket   154
    Sweet Potato Brisket   155
Saucy Miami Ribs With Parsnips   156
    Rib Appetizer   157

Brisket Ends 158
Brisket Boats 159
Smothered Short Ribs 160
Short Rib Chunks With Rice 161
Meatballs With Mushrooms 162
Meatball Mushroom Sloppy Joes 163
Overnight Shabbos Corned Beef 164
Club Sandwiches 165
Taco Bowl Night 166
Taco Dinner 167

DAIRY

Pull-Apart Eggplant Parmesan 170
Baby Eggplant Parmesan 171
Low Cal Cauliflower Mushroom Risotto 172
Risotto Balls 173
Summery Feta Salad 174
Romaine Feta Salad 175
Zoodle Cheese Nests 176
Zoodle Lasagna 177
Crustless Baby Red Potato Quiche 178
Mini Potato Tarts 179
Cheesy Seed Crisps 180
Caesar Crisp Salad 181
Keto Cheese Crust Pizza 182
Individual Pizzas 183
Granola Crusted "Breakfast" Tart 184
Yogurt Parfait 185
Baked Broccoli Tots 186
Broccoli Tart 187
5-Ingredient Cauliflower Cheese Bites 188
Cauliflower Quiche 189
Avocado Pesto Spaghetti 190
Elbow Noodle Pesto 191
Lazy Hash And Egg Dinner 192
Feta Quinoa Hash 193

GRAIN SIDES

Crispy Garlic Couscous 196
Panko Garlic Cherry Tomatoes 197
Jasmine Coconut And Cranberry Rice 198
Coconut Bowls 199
Candied Brown Rice Salad 200
Crunch Topping 201
Mediterranean Quinoa Salad 202
Quinoa Bowl 203
Spicy Roasted Cauliflower And Chickpea Salad 204
Lentil Cauliflower Salad 205
Asian Rice Salad With Wasabi Peas 206
Chinese Box Rice Salad 207
Roasted Onion Quinoa Salad 208
Colorful Quinoa Salad 209
Fresh Orzo Salad 210
Orzo Pepper Cups 211
Crouton Farro Salad 212
Barley Poke Bowl 213

VEGETABLE SIDES

Garlic Shishito Peppers 216
Shishito Board 217
Maple-Glazed Japanese Sweet Potatoes 218
Salad Bowls 219
Lemon-Mint Mini Peppers 220
Roasted Pepper Wraps 221
"Everything Bagel" Asparagus 222
Asparagus And Rice 223
Spiced Eggplant Wedges 224
Hummus Eggplant Topper 225
Pretty Roasted Onion Flowers 226
Onion Garnish 227
Chip-Topped Green Beans 228
Green Bean Salad 229
Herbed Honey-Roasted Tomatoes 230
Cherry Tomato Ramekins 231
Dilled Roasted Cauliflower And Broccoli 232
Shredded Veggie Hash 233
Peanut Butter Sweet Potatoes 234
Sweet Potato Rounds 235
Steamed Broccoli With Ginger Topping 236
Gingery Steamed Cabbage 237

Salted Baby Potatoes 238
  Potato Skewers 239
Hash Brown "Potato Kugel" Waffles 240
  Deli Hash Brown Pizza 241

DESSERT

Double Chocolate Banana Cake 244
  Double Chocolate Muffins 245
Chocolate Covered Chickpeas 246
  Flavored Chocolate Chickpeas 247
Strawberry Almond Tart 248
  Peach Crisps 249
Peanut Butter Chocolate Popcorn 250
  Popcorn Bark 251
Low-Fat Ginger Biscotti 252
  Ginger Berry Cups 253
Mint Chocolate Chip Cookies 254
  Ice Cream Sandwiches 255
Espresso Chocolate Chip Cookies 256
  Mini Espresso Cookies 257
Black And White Moist Chocolate Cake 258
  Mini Cakes 259

Classic Fruit Flan 260
  Lemon Parfait 261
The Blue Cake 262
  Colorful Cakes 263
Coconut Chocolate Tart 264
  Rectangular Coconut Tart 265
Coconut Strawberry Shortcake 266
  Berry Cups 267
Olive Oil Salted Brownies 268
  Brownie Cake 269
Rose Petal Apple Tart 270
  Apple Crisps 271
Afternoon Snack Bars 272
  Granola Balls 273
Cayenne-Lime Mango And Watermelon 274
  Lime Zest Fruit Cups 275
Dragon Fruit Salad 276
  Dragon Fruit Skewers 277
Candied Marshmallow Lollipops 278
  Marshmallow Cake 279

Nutritional Information 280
Index 291

INTRODUCTION

As I sit down to write the introduction to my third cookbook, I am so thankful and overwhelmed by all your support. Writing cookbooks has been the most amazing journey for me. I have been able to turn my hobby into an exciting career, something I will never take for granted. Thank you for supporting me on this three-book journey. I so appreciate the feedback of friends and strangers who find the time to tell me my cookbooks have enriched their lives in the kitchen. I wanted to give my readers and followers the ability to prepare healthy and simple meals for family and friends without compromising on taste or presentation. I wanted to give people the tools to enjoy cooking and not find it a chore or take up too much of their time. Your feedback has been overwhelmingly positive, for which I thank you all so much.

The intention of my first book, *The Silver Platter: Simple to Spectacular*, was to create a cookbook that used basic ingredients. I wanted people to experiment with the simplest of recipes and produce the best results. I wanted to invite readers who were not comfortable in the kitchen to enjoy cooking with ease.

My second book, *The Silver Platter: Simple Elegance*, focused on recipes with a little more creative flair, not in terms of ingredients or complexity, but in presentation and attention to detail. The recipes are just as simple as in my first book, but they have a little something special to make them stand out, whether it's a crunch on a salad or a garnish in a soup. As we all know, we eat with our eyes first, and this book teaches readers how to achieve that.

We learned the basics in my first book, added a creative flair in my second book, and now it's time to have some fun with versatility. All this while staying true to my healthy and simple way of cooking. A recipe will never get old if we are creative with the foods we prepare.

This, my third book, *Variations*, creates versatile recipes that showcase two variations for each prepared food. We learn that recipes don't have to stick within their original boundaries. A chicken dish can be prepared as a main or as an appetizer, a family-style salad can be served individually, and a batch of cookies can become a large cookie cake. The possibilities are endless, and my goal is for creativity within each recipe.

Each recipe in this book includes a variation on the right-hand page. These "Variation" recipes present a different way to showcase the main recipe; they often include additional ingredients, shown in bold type, to make a completely new dish. The photo on each page displays both the main recipe and the variation, so you can see how each of them will look after you have prepared them.

I am not a chef. What I like to call myself is a creative cook. I enjoy using simple ingredients, color, and texture, while incorporating versatility. I am so excited to share this new cookbook with everyone. I hope it redefines how we think about cooking and allows people to be more creative.

I appreciate and thank you for all for your support and help over the years. If you have questions, please reach out to me on social media (Daniella Silver cooks on Facebook or daniellasilvercooks on instagram). I love to hear from you.

Thank you again.

XO
Daniella

"A MAJOR GOAL OF MY COOKBOOKS IS TO ALLOW PEOPLE TO ENJOY THEIR LIVES AND NOT BE BOGGED DOWN BY COOKING."

XO
Daniella

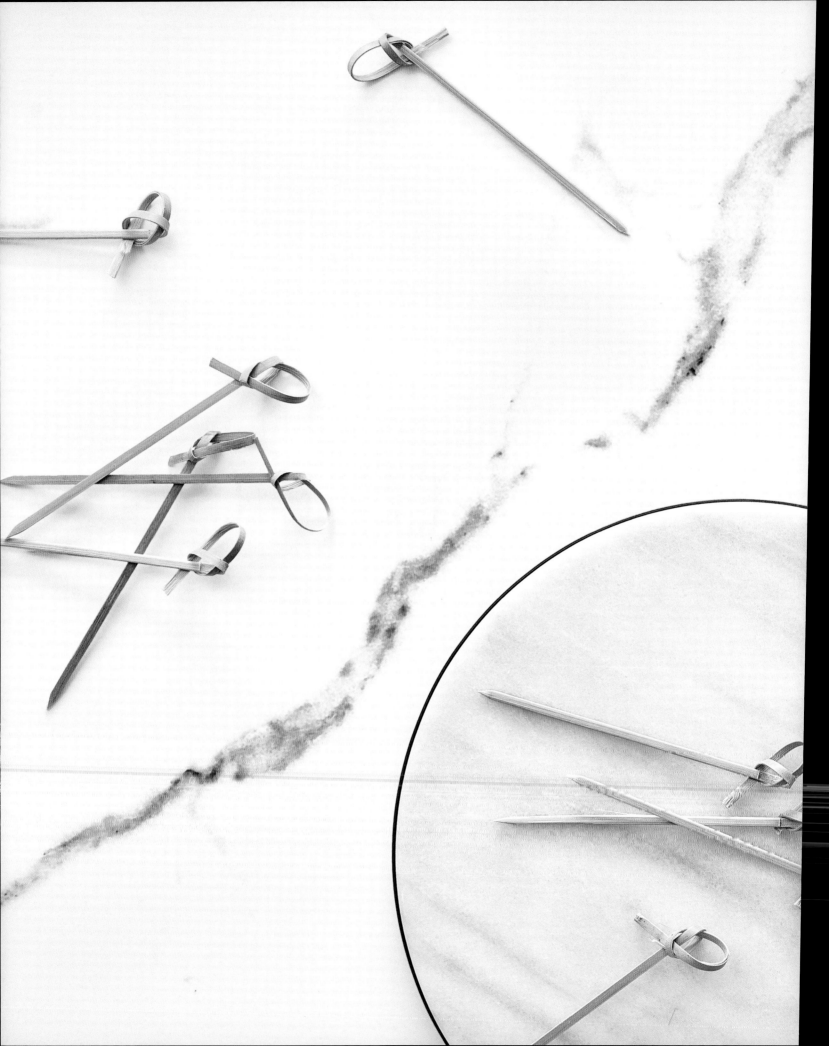

APPETIZERS

Corned Beef Topped Eggplant

MEAT I GLUTEN-FREE I MEAT FREEZES WELL I YIELDS 4-6 SERVINGS

INGREDIENTS

1 large eggplant
*trimmed and cut
into 1-inch rounds*

kosher salt

black pepper

3-4 Tbsp extra light olive oil,
divided

1 lb/500 g deli corned beef
*thinly sliced, cut into
bite-size pieces*

1 large onion
diced

2 Tbsp soy sauce or tamari

2 Tbsp honey

2 Tbsp fresh
chopped parsley
for garnish

METHOD

1   Preheat oven to 350°F. Line
a rimmed baking sheet with
parchment paper.

2   Arrange eggplant rounds in
a single layer on prepared
baking sheet. Sprinkle with
salt and pepper; drizzle with
2 tablespoons oil.

3   Bake, uncovered, for 30-35 minutes or until tender.

4   Meanwhile, in a skillet or frying pan, heat remaining oil. Sauté corned beef and onions for 3-5 minutes, until onions have softened.

5   Stir in soy sauce and honey; sauté for 5 minutes.

6   Arrange baked eggplant rounds on a serving platter. Spoon on corned beef mixture; garnish with parsley.

VARIATION

INDIVIDUAL EGGPLANT ROUNDS

Prepare recipe as directed, but serve eggplant rounds and topping on individual plates.

Turkey-Wrapped Enoki Mushrooms

MEAT I GLUTEN-FREE I YIELDS 4-6 SERVINGS

INGREDIENTS

2 bunches (6 oz/170 g each)
enoki mushrooms
stems trimmed

20 slices deli turkey

1 Tbsp extra light olive oil

2 Tbsp honey

2 Tbsp soy sauce or tamari

METHOD

1   Preheat oven to 400°F. Line
a rimmed baking sheet with
parchment paper.

2   Separate a small bouquet of 10-15 mushroom strands. Place 1 slice of turkey on a work surface; place mushroom bouquet onto turkey and roll up tightly, with mushroom tops exposed. Place rolls onto prepared baking sheet, seam-side down.

3   In a small bowl, combine oil, honey, and soy sauce; mix well.

4   Using a silicone brush, brush each roll from top to bottom.

5   Bake, uncovered, for 10-15 minutes, or until lightly golden.

VARIATION

TURKEY WRAPS ON SALAD

Prepare recipe as directed. For a cute appetizer idea, serve 2 turkey rolls with a **side salad** or **Rainbow Bright Salad**, (p. 80).

Sesame Seed Rice Balls

PAREVE I GLUTEN-FREE I YIELDS 12-15 BALLS

INGREDIENTS

1 cup sushi rice

1 cup water

1 tsp kosher salt

2 Tbsp black sesame seeds

2 Tbsp white sesame seeds

DIPPING SAUCE

spicy mayo

sriracha or hot sauce

METHOD

1   In a medium pot, combine rice with water and salt. Bring to a boil over high heat. Reduce heat to low, cover pot, and simmer for about 15 minutes, or until water is absorbed. Let cool

2   Combine sesame seeds into a medium bowl.
    Wet your hands; roll rice into 2-inch balls.
    Coat balls on all sides with sesame seed
    mixture. Place onto platter.

3   Serve with dipping sauce of your choice.

VARIATION

FRIED RICE BALLS

Prepare rice as directed. Place 1 cup
of **panko crumbs** (gluten-free or
regular) into a medium bowl. Coat
balls in panko crumbs. Heat **oil** in a
frying pan over medium-high heat.
Working in batches, fry balls on all
sides, until brown and crunchy. Serve
with suggested dipping sauces.

Deli-Wrapped Squash Bites

MEAT I PASSOVER I GLUTEN-FREE I YIELDS 6-8 SERVINGS

INGREDIENTS

2 cups butternut squash
cut into 1-inch cubes
(precut squash works well)

kosher salt

black pepper

**10-15 slices deli
corned beef**
cut in half widthwise

1 tsp chili powder
(or to taste)

1 tsp garlic powder

2 Tbsp brown sugar

SPECIAL EQUIPMENT

20-30 toothpicks

METHOD

1 Preheat oven to 375°F. Line
a rimmed baking sheet with
parchment paper.

2 Submerge toothpicks in a
small bowl of water; soak for
about 5 minutes.

3   Sprinkle squash cubes with salt and pepper. Wrap each squash cube with a half-slice of corned beef, overlapping it on the bottom side, if necessary.

4   Fasten with a toothpick. Arrange wrapped cubes in a single layer on prepared baking sheet.

5   In a small bowl, combine chili powder, garlic powder, and brown sugar; mix well. Sprinkle over corned beef.

6   Bake, uncovered, for about 30 minutes, until squash is tender and meat is glazed and golden.

VARIATION

SQUASH BITES ON SPOONS

Follow recipe as directed. Place cubes onto individual mini spoons and remove toothpicks. Great alongside a **side salad**, as well.

Great for a party.

Crunchy Chicken Kale Salad

MEAT I GLUTEN-FREE I YIELDS 4-6 SERVINGS

INGREDIENTS

1 bunch kale
(about 1 lb/500 g)

2 cups diced or shredded
boneless cooked chicken

4 Israeli pickles
trimmed and cut into rounds

1 firm ripe Hass avocado

½ cup sunflower seeds or
pumpkin seeds

1 cup crushed potato chips
or terra chips

DRESSING

⅓ cup extra light olive oil

3 Tbsp apple cider vinegar

3 Tbsp honey

2 cloves garlic
minced (about 1 tsp)

⅓ cup diced red onion

¼ cup chopped fresh dill

kosher salt

black pepper

METHOD

1   Wash and dry kale. Remove
     and discard tough stalks and
     center ribs. Tear leaves into
     bite-size pieces; you should
     have about 8 cups. Place kale
     into a large bowl; massage
     with your fingertips until
     leaves have wilted, about 5
     minutes.

2   Add chicken and pickles.
     Cover and refrigerate.

3   Dressing: Combine dressing ingredients
    in a glass jar; seal tightly and shake well.
    Refrigerate.

4   Shortly before serving, peel, pit, and dice
    avocado. Add to bowl along with sunflower
    seeds. Gently toss with dressing to combine.
    Scatter crushed chips over salad. Serve
    chilled.

VARIATION

CHICKEN KALE WRAPS

Wash and dry kale. Cut kale leaves in
half, discarding tough center rib. Top
with chicken, pickles, avocado slices,
sunflower seeds, and chips. Drizzle
with dressing. Serve on individual
plates. Fold kale around toppings to
form a wrap. Enjoy!

Deli Egg Rolls

MEAT I GLUTEN-FREE OPTION I EGG ROLLS FREEZE WELL I YIELDS 8-10 SERVINGS

INGREDIENTS

1 lb/500 g sliced
deli corned beef

1 lb/500 g sliced deli turkey

2 ripe Hass avocados
halved, pitted, and thinly sliced

2 cups shredded spinach

8-10 large egg roll
wrappers

oil
for frying

HONEY DIJON DIPPING SAUCE

3 Tbsp extra light olive oil

3 Tbsp honey

1 Tbsp Dijon mustard

1 Tbsp apple cider vinegar

METHOD

1   Line a large tray with
    parchment paper; set aside.
    Place corned beef, turkey,
    avocados, and spinach into
    separate bowls.

2   Layer slices of corned
    beef, turkey, avocado, and
    shredded spinach onto an
    egg roll wrapper, leaving a
    1-inch border on all sides.
    Do not overfill. Lift bottom
    edge of wrapper over filling,
    then fold in sides and roll up
    tightly. Place seam-side down
    on prepared tray. Repeat.

3   In a large heavy-bottomed saucepan, heat oil. Fry egg rolls for 2-3 minutes per side, until golden. Drain on paper towels.

4   Dipping Sauce: Place all dipping sauce ingredients into a small bowl; mix well.

5   To serve, slice each roll on the diagonal; arrange on individual plates or a serving platter. Serve with dipping sauce.

VARIATION

DELI RICE PAPER ROLLS

Fill a pie plate with lukewarm water. Working with one **rice paper wrapper** at a time, immerse it in water for 5-7 seconds or until pliable. (Be careful, as they tear easily.) Place onto a clean towel; pat dry. Layer filling ingredients on rice paper. Roll up as instructed in Step 2. Repeat with remaining ingredients. Great for a gluten-free diet.

Corned Beef Biscotti

MEAT I GLUTEN-FREE OPTION I FREEZES WELL I YIELDS 2-3 DOZEN

INGREDIENTS

½ cup vegetable oil

2 eggs

½ cup sugar

1 tsp pure vanilla extract

20 slices deli corned beef
cut into bite-size pieces

2⅓ cups flour
(or gluten-free flour)

1 tsp baking soda

pinch kosher salt

METHOD

1   Preheat oven to 350°F. Line a rimmed baking sheet with parchment paper.

2   In a large mixing bowl, whisk together oil, eggs, sugar, and vanilla until well blended. Add corned beef.

3   Stir in flour, baking soda, and salt.

4   Transfer dough to prepared baking sheet; shape into two long narrow logs (about 1½ inches wide). Bake for 30-35 minutes, or until lightly golden.

5   Reduce oven temperature to 300°F. Using a serrated knife, cut logs into slices about ¾-inch thick. Turn slices cut side up. Bake for 25-30 minutes, until golden and crisp. Transfer to an appetizer meat board before serving. Refrigerate any leftover biscotti.

VARIATION

BEEF-WRAPPED BISCOTTI

Prepare biscotti as directed. Using additional **corned beef**, wrap 1 slice around the middle of each twice-baked biscotti for a pretty and tasty presentation. Refrigerate any leftover biscotti and corned beef.

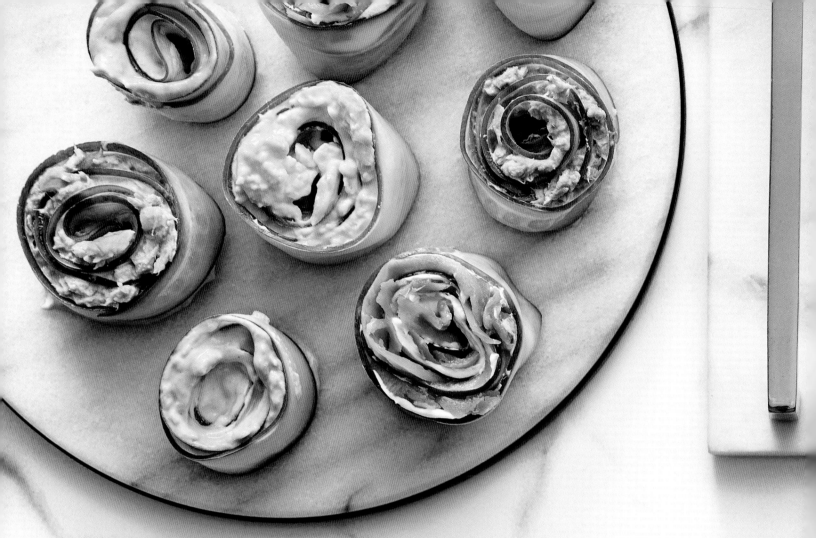

Cucumber Roll Ups

DAIRY, MEAT, OR PAREVE I GLUTEN-FREE I YIELDS 4 SERVINGS

INGREDIENTS

1-2 large English cucumber
trimmed (do not peel)

DAIRY FILLING OPTION

½ cup cream cheese

¼ lb smoked salmon

MEAT FILLING OPTION

½ cup chopped liver

PAREVE FILLING OPTIONS

½ cup hummus
(store-bought or homemade)

½ cup egg salad
(store-bought or homemade)

METHOD

1   Using a vegetable peeler, slice sides of cucumber lengthwise into 4-5 thin strips per side, forming long ribbons. Reserve cucumber centers for another use.

2   Place cucumber ribbons onto a paper towel; pat dry.

3   Spread a thin coat of desired filling along
    the length of each cucumber ribbon, coating
    it from top to bottom so it adheres when
    rolled up.

4   Starting from one end, roll cucumber ribbon
    into a pinwheel — no toothpick should be
    needed. Repeat with remaining cucumbers
    and filling. Serve immediately.

VARIATION

CUCUMBER BOATS

Trim 1-2 large cucumbers. Cut about
3-4 inches into "boats" and scoop out
seeds. Fill cucumbers with preferred
filling.

Zaatar Avocado

PAREVE I GLUTEN-FREE I YIELDS 4-6 SERVINGS

INGREDIENTS

2 ripe avocados

8 skewers

zaatar

METHOD

1 Peel and quarter avocados.
   Cut each quarter into thirds.

2 Thread 3 pieces of avocado
   onto skewers. Sprinkle with
   zaatar.

3 Place skewers onto a platter.
   Serve immediately.

VARIATION

AVOCADO SLICES / GUACAMOLE

Peel and pit avocados; cut into thin slices. Place onto serving platter. Top with zaatar. Alternatively, make a dip by mashing avocados and topping with zaatar.

Cute Baguette Cups

PAREVE I GLUTEN-FREE OPTION I YIELDS 4 SERVINGS

INGREDIENTS

1 *(10-inch)* **long white baguette**
(gluten-free or regular)

4 carrots
trimmed, peeled, and cut in half crosswise and then lengthwise

4 baby cucumbers
trimmed, cut in half crosswise and then lengthwise

1 cup fresh broccoli

1 cup halved cherry tomatoes

OPTIONAL FILLINGS

½ cup hummus
(store-bought or homemade)

½ cup egg salad
(store-bought or homemade)

½ cup salsa
(store-bought or homemade)

½ cup tuna salad
(store-bought or homemade)

METHOD

1   Trim ends of baguette. Slice baguette into 6-7 pieces, each 2-3 inches thick.

2   Using your thumb, gently push down the center of each bread slice, forming a cup. Make sure not to push completely through.

3   Scoop 1-2 tablespoons desired filling into each
    bread cup.

4   Create an assortment of 3-4 veggies and
    stand them up in the filling. Arrange on a
    platter; serve immediately.

VARIATION

BREAD CUP IDEAS

For a variation, use a **black bread
or whole wheat baguette.** Also
change up some of the veggies, such
as 1 bunch **asparagus**, parboiled and
halved; 1 **red bell pepper**, trimmed,
cut in half crosswise and then
lengthwise; or **celery**, cut into sticks.
For additional filling options, try ½
cup **eggplant dip**, and, for a **meat
option**, use ½ cup **chopped liver**.

Lemon Herbed Bone Marrow

MEAT I GLUTEN-FREE OPTION I YIELDS 4-6 SERVINGS

INGREDIENTS

8 bone marrow bones

kosher salt

black pepper

1 cup unseasoned
panko crumbs
(gluten-free or regular)

2 Tbsp extra light olive oil

2 Tbsp pure maple syrup

2 tsp lemon zest

¼ cup chopped
fresh parsley

METHOD

1   Preheat oven to 400°F.
    Coat a 9 x 13-inch glass or
    ceramic baking dish with
    nonstick cooking spray.

2   Arrange bones in a single
    layer in prepared baking dish.
    Sprinkle generously with salt
    and pepper.

3 In a small bowl, combine panko with oil, maple syrup, lemon zest, and parsley; mix well.

4 Spoon panko mixture evenly over bones. Bake, uncovered, for 15-20 minutes, or until crumbs are browned and crisp.

VARIATION

BONE MARROW SPREAD

Prepare recipe as directed. Serve alongside **crostini**; scoop out marrow to spread on crostini, or place onto deli board with sliced **deli**, **pickles**, and **olives**.

Dill Pickle Football Wings

MEAT I PASSOVER I GLUTEN-FREE I WINGS FREEZE WELL I YIELDS 4-6 SERVINGS

INGREDIENTS

2 dozen chicken wings

1 cup dill pickle juice

2 Tbsp honey

½ cup chopped fresh dill
plus more for garnish

2-3 Tbsp extra light olive oil

5-6 medium dill pickles
trimmed and quartered,
for garnish

METHOD

1   In a large resealable bag,
    combine chicken wings
    with pickle juice, honey, dill,
    and oil. Marinate for 20-30
    minutes (or overnight in the
    refrigerator).

2   Preheat oven to 400°F. Line
    a large rimmed baking sheet
    with parchment paper.

3   Remove wings from marinade; discard
    marinade. Arrange wings in a single layer on
    prepared baking sheet.

4   Bake, uncovered, for 30-40 minutes, until
    crispy and cooked through.

5   Transfer to a serving platter; garnish with
    sliced pickles and sprinkle with additional dill.

VARIATION

PICKLE CHICKEN BITES

Cut 6 pieces white or dark **chicken
cutlets** into 2-inch pieces. Marinate
as directed in Step 1. Remove from
marinade; place onto a baking sheet.
Bake, uncovered, for 20-30 minutes,
until browned. Place on a serving
platter; top each with a **pickle slice**,
and fasten with a toothpick.

SOUPS

Healing Celery Soup

PAREVE I PASSOVER I GLUTEN-FREE I FREEZES WELL I YIELDS 6-8 SERVINGS

INGREDIENTS

2 Tbsp extra light olive oil

1 large onion
diced

4 cloves garlic
minced (about 2 tsp)

6 cups celery
trimmed and sliced

2 Yukon potatoes
peeled, cut into chunks

5-6 cups vegetable broth
or water

1 bay leaf

1½ tsp kosher salt
or to taste

black pepper

¼ cup chopped fresh dill
plus more for garnish

¼ cup chopped fresh parsley
plus more for garnish

METHOD

1   Heat oil in a large soup pot
over medium heat. Add
onion and garlic; sauté for
5-7 minutes, until softened.

2   Add celery, potatoes, broth,
bay leaf, salt, pepper, dill,
and parsley. Bring to a boil.

3   Reduce heat. Simmer, partially covered, for
    30-40 minutes or until vegetables are tender,
    stirring occasionally. Remove from heat; let
    cool slightly. Discard bay leaf.

4   Using an immersion blender, process soup
    until smooth. If soup is too thick, add a little
    water. Adjust seasonings to taste. Garnish
    with additional herbs.

VARIATION

REFRESHING CELERY SOUP

Prepare recipe as directed. Let cool
to room temperature or refrigerate.
Serve as an appetizer in shot
glasses at room temperature or as a
cold soup.

Sweet Potato Pear Soup

PAREVE I PASSOVER I GLUTEN-FREE I FREEZES WELL I YIELDS 8-10 SERVINGS

INGREDIENTS

2 Tbsp extra light olive oil

1 large onion, diced

2 ribs celery, chopped

2 cloves garlic
minced (about 1 tsp)

kosher salt

black pepper

4 large sweet potatoes
peeled and chopped

3 Asian or Bosc pears
peeled and chopped

1 tsp sweet paprika

pinch dried thyme

5-6 cups water or
vegetable broth

METHOD

1   Heat oil in a large soup pot
    over medium heat. Add
    onion, celery, garlic, salt,
    and pepper; sauté for 8-10
    minutes, until golden.

2   Add sweet potatoes, pears,
    paprika, thyme, and water.
    Bring to a boil.

3   Reduce heat. Simmer, partially covered, for 40-45 minutes, or until vegetables are tender, stirring occasionally. Remove from heat; let cool slightly.

4   Using an immersion blender, process soup until smooth. If soup is too thick, add a little water. Adjust seasonings to taste.

VARIATION

CINNAMON SUGAR PEARS

Prepare soup as directed. Preheat oven to 400°F. Coat a cooking rack or pizza tray with nonstick cooking spray. Slice 2 additional **pears** very thinly (do not peel). Sprinkle with **sugar** and **cinnamon** on both sides. Bake, uncovered, for 20-25 minutes until golden. Garnish the soup with baked pears or sprinkle soup with **thyme leaves.**

Toasted Garlic Panko Topping

PAREVE | GLUTEN-FREE OPTION |
YIELDS 6-8 SERVINGS

INGREDIENTS

1 cup panko *(gluten-free or regular)*

1 tsp onion powder

1 tsp garlic powder

1 tsp kosher salt

2 Tbsp extra light olive oil

METHOD

1   In a large frying pan, combine all
    ingredients; toast mixture on medium high
    heat for 3-5 minutes, until golden.

2   Sprinkle over soup at serving time.

Crunchy Seed Topping

PAREVE | GLUTEN-FREE |
YIELDS 6-8 SERVINGS

INGREDIENTS

⅓ cup salted   1 Tbsp black
sunflower seeds   sesame seeds

⅓ cup pumpkin seeds   2 Tbsp honey

1 Tbsp white   2 Tbsp extra light
sesame seeds   olive oil

METHOD

1   Preheat oven to 375°F. Line a rimmed baking
    sheet with parchment paper.

2   In a medium bowl, combine all ingredients.

3   Spread in a single layer on prepared baking
    sheet. Bake, uncovered, for 12-15 minutes,
    until crunchy.

4   Sprinkle over soup at serving time.

Spiced Popcorn Topping

PAREVE I GLUTEN-FREE I
YIELDS 6-8 SERVINGS

INGREDIENTS

2 cups popped popcorn

1 tsp kosher salt

1 tsp sweet paprika

1 tsp zaatar

METHOD

1   In a large bowl, combine popcorn with
    salt, paprika, and zaatar; mix well.

2   Sprinkle over soup at serving time.

Chunky Mushroom Soup

PAREVE I GLUTEN-FREE I FREEZES WELL I YIELDS 8 SERVINGS

INGREDIENTS

2 Tbsp extra light olive oil

1 large onion
diced

4 cloves garlic
minced (about 2 tsp)

4 cups halved button
mushrooms

4 cups sliced Portobello
mushrooms

4 cups sliced shiitake
mushrooms

1 bunch (6 oz/ 170 g each)
enoki mushrooms
trimmed and separated

3 Tbsp soy sauce or tamari

5-6 cups vegetable broth
or water

2 tsp kosher salt
or to taste

black pepper

⅓ cup fresh minced parsley

METHOD

1   Heat oil in a large soup pot
    over medium heat. Add
    onion and garlic; sauté for
    5-7 minutes, until golden.

2   Add mushrooms, soy sauce,
    broth, salt, and pepper; bring
    to a boil.

3 Reduce heat. Simmer, partially covered, for
   20-25 minutes or until mushrooms are tender,
   stirring occasionally. Adjust seasonings to
   taste. Top with fresh parsley.

VARIATION

PUREED MUSHROOM SOUP

Follow recipe as directed. Using an
immersion blender, process soup until
pureed. Garnish with additional fresh
parsley.

Spiralized Noodle Soup

MEAT OR PAREVE I PASSOVER I GLUTEN-FREE I YIELDS 8-10 SERVINGS

INGREDIENTS

2 Tbsp extra light olive oil

1 large onion
diced

4 cloves garlic
minced (about 2 tsp)

8-10 cups chicken broth or
vegetable broth

1 Tbsp kosher salt
or to taste

black pepper

1 container (12 oz/340 g)
sweet potato spirals

1 container (12 oz/340 g)
zucchini spirals

1 container (12 oz/340 g)
carrot spirals

METHOD

1   Heat oil in a large soup pot
over medium heat. Add
onion and garlic; sauté for
5-7 minutes.

2 Add broth, salt and pepper; bring to a boil. Shortly before serving, reduce heat and add spiralized vegetables; simmer, partially covered, for 3-5 minutes. (There is no need to cut them as the strands will break apart during cooking.) Do not overcook. Adjust seasonings to taste.

VARIATION

ZOODLE CHICKEN SOUP

Prepare recipe as directed in Step 1. Add 8-10 cups **water** and **4-6 boneless chicken cutlets** (white or dark). Bring to a boil. Reduce heat; simmer, partially covered, for 2 hours until cooked through. Shortly before serving, add spiralized veggies; simmer for 3-5 minutes. (Do not overcook. Adjust seasonings to taste. You can shred the chicken for another look.

Healthy Tomato Lentil Soup

PAREVE I GLUTEN-FREE I FREEZES WELL I YIELDS 4-6 SERVINGS

INGREDIENTS

1 cup dried brown lentils
rinsed and drained

4 medium carrots
trimmed and sliced

2 cloves garlic
minced (about 1 tsp)

1 medium onion
trimmed and diced

6 cups water or broth

1 can (6 oz/170 ml)
tomato paste

**¼ cup chopped
fresh parsley**
plus more for garnish

½ tsp dried thyme

1 Tbsp lemon juice
(preferably fresh)

2 tsp kosher salt
or to taste

½ tsp black pepper

METHOD

1   In large soup pot, stir
together lentils, carrots,
garlic, onion, water, tomato
paste, parsley, thyme, lemon
juice, salt, and pepper; bring
to a boil.

2   Reduce heat; simmer,
partially covered, for 30-
40 minutes, or until lentils
are tender. Add more
water or broth if needed.
Do not overcook or lentils
will become mushy. Adjust
seasonings to taste.

VARIATION

MASON JAR LENTIL SOUP

Prepare recipe as directed. Place into medium mason jars and take for lunch at room temperature, or serve them to your guests as a pretty appetizer.

Vegetarian Vegetable Quinoa Soup

PAREVE I PASSOVER I GLUTEN-FREE I FREEZES WELL I YIELDS 8 SERVINGS

INGREDIENTS

2 Tbsp extra light olive oil

1 large onion
diced

4 cloves garlic
minced (about 2 tsp)

2 ribs celery
chopped

2 carrots
peeled and sliced

1 medium zucchini
trimmed and diced

1 large sweet potato
peeled and diced

5-6 cups vegetable broth

2 tsp kosher salt
or to taste

black pepper

2½ cups water

1 cup quinoa

METHOD

1 Heat oil in a large soup pot over medium heat. Add onion and garlic; sauté for 8-10 minutes, until golden.

2 Add celery, carrots, zucchini, sweet potato, broth, salt, and pepper. Bring to a boil.

3 Reduce heat. Simmer, partially covered, for 30-40 minutes or until vegetables are tender, stirring occasionally.

4   Meanwhile, bring water to a boil in a medium saucepan over high heat. Add quinoa; reduce heat. Simmer, covered, for 15 minutes, or until tender. Remove from heat; let stand for 10 minutes, covered. Fluff quinoa with a fork.

5   Spoon soup into individual bowls; add 3-4 tablespoons quinoa; stir to combine.

VARIATION

SHREDDED VEGETABLE SOUP

Using a hand-held shredder or food processor, shred vegetables as listed. Bring vegetable broth to a boil. Shortly before serving, add shredded vegetables; simmer for 5-7 minutes, until tender crisp. Spoon in cooked quinoa; serve immediately.

Broccoli Soup with Caramelized Leeks

PAREVE I PASSOVER I GLUTEN-FREE I FREEZES WELL I YIELDS 4-6 SERVING

INGREDIENTS

2 Tbsp extra light olive oil

2 bunches leeks
(about 6 leeks) trimmed
and thinly sliced

4 cloves garlic
minced (about 2 tsp)

1 head broccoli
fresh or frozen, cut into florets
(about 6 cups)

2 Tbsp honey

2 tsp kosher salt

black pepper

5-6 cups water or
vegetable broth

METHOD

1 Heat oil in a large soup pot
over medium heat. Add leeks
and garlic; sauté for 8-10
minutes, until caramelized.

2 Add broccoli, honey, salt,
pepper, and water. Bring to
a boil.

3   Reduce heat. Simmer, partially covered, for
    30-40 minutes or until vegetables are tender,
    stirring occasionally. Remove from heat; let
    cool slightly.

4   Using an immersion blender, process soup
    until smooth. If soup is too thick, add a little
    water. Adjust seasonings to taste.

VARIATION

CAULIFLOWER SOUP WITH CARAMELIZED LEEKS

Prepare recipe as directed, using
1 head **cauliflower**, fresh or frozen,
broken into florets, in place of
broccoli.

Roasted Kabocha Squash Soup

PAREVE I SOUP GLUTEN-FREE I FREEZES WELL I YIELDS 8 SERVINGS

INGREDIENTS

2 kabocha squash
(about 2-3 lb each),
cut in half, seeded

kosher salt

black pepper

2 Tbsp extra light olive oil

1 large onion
trimmed and diced

2 cloves garlic
minced (about 1 tsp)

1 Tbsp fresh ginger
minced

1 tsp ground cumin

2 tsp honey

5-6 cups water or
vegetable broth

METHOD

1 Preheat oven to 375°F. Line
   a rimmed baking sheet with
   parchment paper.

2 Place squash, cut-side down
   on prepared baking sheet.
   Bake, uncovered, for 35-40
   minutes or until tender. Let
   cool slightly.

3 Meanwhile, heat oil in a large
   soup pot over medium heat.
   Add onion and garlic; sauté
   for 6-8 minutes, or until
   golden.

4 Scoop out squash pulp; add to onion mixture.
   Discard squash peels.

5 Add ginger, cumin, honey, and water. Bring to
   a boil. Reduce heat; simmer, partially covered,
   for 20-25 minutes.

6 Using an immersion blender, process soup
   until smooth. If soup is too thick, add a little
   water or broth. Adjust seasonings to taste.

VARIATION

SOUP BREAD BOWLS

Prepare recipe as directed. Hollow
out 8 large **bread rolls**, making sure
not to cut through to the bottom,
reserving middle for croutons. Cut
reserved bread into cubes; toast in
oven until crisp. Right before serving,
spoon soup into bowls, almost to
the top. Garnish with toasted bread;
serve immediately.

Great for holidays and special
occasions.

Dinner Steak Soup

MEAT I GLUTEN-FREE I FREEZES WELL I YIELDS 8 SERVINGS

INGREDIENTS

1 Tbsp extra light olive oil

2 lb skirt steak
cut into 2-inch pieces

1 medium onion
diced

2 large carrot
trimmed and diced

2 cloves garlic
minced (about 1 tsp)

¼ cup tomato paste

5-6 cups water or
chicken broth

1 bay leaf

1 cup fresh or
frozen corn kernels

1 can (19 oz/540 ml) white
beans or black beans

2 tsp kosher salt
or to taste

black pepper

METHOD

1   Heat oil in a large soup pot
over medium-high heat. Add
steak, cook until browned,
5-7 minutes. Stir in onion,
carrots, and garlic; cook 5-7
minutes, until softened.

2   Add tomato paste, water, and bay leaf; bring to a boil. Reduce heat; simmer, partially covered, for about 30 minutes, until beef is tender.

3   Add corn and beans; simmer for 40 minutes. Season with salt and pepper. Discard bay leaf before serving.

VARIATION

TOFU SOUP

Prepare recipe as directed, replacing meat with **extra-firm tofu** that has been cut into 1-inch-thick chunks. You can also add 1 can of **chickpeas** (19 oz /540 g), rinsed and drained, to boost the protein.

SALADS

Simply Sweet Mini Pepper Salad

PAREVE | GLUTEN-FREE | YIELDS 6 SERVINGS

INGREDIENTS

2 pkgs (14-16 oz each)
mini sweet peppers
(assorted colors)

⅓ cup **red onion**
thinly sliced

½ cup **fresh dill**
minced

DRESSING

⅓ cup extra light olive oil

3 Tbsp balsamic vinegar

2 tsp honey

1 tsp Dijon mustard

2 cloves garlic
minced (about 1 tsp)

pinch kosher salt

black pepper

METHOD

1   Core, seed, and slice peppers
    into rounds. Place into a
    medium bowl. Add onion and
    dill. Cover; refrigerate.

2   Dressing: Combine dressing
    ingredients in a glass jar;
    seal tightly and shake well.
    Refrigerate.

3   Shortly before serving, toss
    salad with dressing.

VARIATION

PEPPERS 'N DIP

Wash and dry peppers well (do not trim tops). Arrange peppers slightly leaning on each other on a wooden or marble board or serving platter. Shake dressing in a glass jar until well blended; pour into a small bowl or keep in the glass jar; place on the prepared board as a dipping sauce. Serve immediately.

Great for a party appetizer or to keep on your counter for a healthy snack.

Pea Shoot Salad

PAREVE I GLUTEN-FREE I YIELDS 6-8 SERVINGS

INGREDIENTS

2 cups sugar snap peas
trimmed, cut into 1-inch pieces

2 cups snow peas
trimmed, cut into 1-inch pieces

1 cup shelled green peas or edamame beans

1 container (1 lb/120 g) pea shoots or pea sprouts
trimmed, cut into 1-inch strands

3 scallions
thinly sliced

¾ cup dried cranberries

DRESSING

⅓ cup extra light olive oil

3 Tbsp rice vinegar

2 Tbsp soy sauce or tamari

3 Tbsp honey

⅓ cup chopped fresh basil

kosher salt
to taste

black pepper

METHOD

1   In a large salad bowl, combine sugar snap peas, snow peas, green peas, pea shoots, scallions, and dried cranberries. Cover, refrigerate.

2   Dressing: Combine dressing ingredients in a glass jar; seal tightly and shake well. Refrigerate.

3   Before serving, toss salad with dressing.

VARIATION

MASON JAR SALAD

Prepare recipe as directed. Place dressed salad into small or large mason jars.

Take for lunch the next day or serve individually as an appetizer in the mini mason jars.

Fresh Herb Granola Salad

PAREVE | GLUTEN-FREE OPTION | YIELD 6 SERVINGS

INGREDIENTS

GRANOLA TOPPING

1 cup large flake oats
(regular or gluten-free)

½ cup slivered or
sliced almonds

1 Tbsp extra light olive oil

pinch kosher salt

SALAD

6 stalks celery
trimmed and thinly sliced

1½ bunches flat leaf parsley
roughly chopped

2 scallions
thinly sliced

¾ cup dried cranberries

DRESSING

⅓ cup extra light olive oil

⅓ cup fresh lemon juice

1 Tbsp honey

kosher salt

black pepper

METHOD

1   Preheat oven to 350° F. Line
a rimmed baking sheet with
parchment paper.

2   Granola Topping: In a
medium bowl, combine oats,
almonds, oil, and salt; mix
to combine. Spread evenly
on prepared baking sheet.
Bake, uncovered, for 12-18
minutes, until lightly toasted.
Remove from oven; let cool.

3   Salad: In a large salad bowl,
toss together celery, parsley,
scallions, and cranberries.
Cover; refrigerate.

4   Dressing: Combine dressing ingredients in a glass jar; seal tightly and shake well.

5   Shortly before serving, toss salad together with dressing. Sprinkle with granola topping; toss lightly to combine.

VARIATION

ENDIVE BOAT SALAD

Prepare recipe as directed. Serve in individual **endive lettuce** cups.

Avocado Lentil Salad

PAREVE I GLUTEN-FREE I YIELDS 4-6 SERVINGS

INGREDIENTS

2 cans (19 oz/540 ml each)
brown lentils
drained, rinsed, and patted dry

2 **scallions**
thinly sliced

½ cup minced **fresh dill**

1 cup **cherry tomatoes**
halved

2 ripe **Hass avocados**

DRESSING

⅓ cup **extra light olive oil**

⅓ cup **lime juice**
(preferably fresh)

1 Tbsp **Dijon mustard**

2 cloves **garlic**
minced (about 1 tsp)

1 tsp **kosher salt**

black pepper

METHOD

1   In a medium bowl, combine
    lentils with scallions, dill,
    and cherry tomatoes. Cover;
    refrigerate.

2   Dressing: Combine dressing
    ingredients in a glass jar;
    seal tightly and shake well.
    Refrigerate.

3   Shortly before serving,
    peel, pit, and dice avocados.
    Add to lentils. Gently stir in
    dressing.

VARIATION

AVOCADO BOWLS

Cut 2-4 avocados in half; remove pits. Follow Steps 1-2. Spoon about ¼-cup lentil salad onto each avocado, filling the cavity and mounding it on the surface. Serve as a plated appetizer.

Panko-Topped Kale Salad

PAREVE I GLUTEN-FREE OPTION I YIELDS 8 SERVINGS

INGREDIENTS

TOPPING

¾ cup unseasoned panko crumbs (regular or gluten-free)

⅓ cup sliced almonds

½ tsp kosher salt

¼ tsp black pepper

½ tsp onion powder

1-2 Tbsp extra light olive oil

SALAD

1 medium bunch kale

4 scallions
thinly sliced

1 cup cherry tomatoes
halved

DRESSING

⅔ cup extra light olive oil

2 Tbsp balsamic vinegar

2 Tbsp white wine vinegar

2 tsp Dijon mustard

2 Tbsp honey

kosher salt

black pepper

METHOD

1   Preheat oven to 350°F. Line a rimmed baking sheet with parchment paper.

2   In a medium bowl, combine panko crumbs with almonds, salt, pepper, onion powder, and oil; mix well.

3   Spread panko mixture in a single layer on prepared baking sheet. Bake, uncovered, for 15-20 minutes, until golden.

VARIATION

4   Wash and dry kale. Remove and discard tough stalks and ribs. Tear leaves into bite-size pieces to make about 8 cups. Place kale into a large bowl; massage with your fingertips until leaves have wilted, about 5 minutes.

5   Add scallions and cherry tomatoes. Cover; refrigerate.

6   Dressing: Combine dressing ingredients in a glass jar; seal tightly and shake well. Refrigerate.

7   Shortly before serving, toss salad together with dressing. Sprinkle with toasted panko mixture and toss lightly to combine.

KALE RICE ROLLS

Prepare recipe as directed. See page 25 for instructions on preparing rice paper wrappers.

Arrange a layer of tossed salad onto a **rice paper wrapper**, leaving a 1-inch border on all sides. Do not overfill. Lift bottom edge of wrapper over filling; fold in sides and roll up tightly. Place seam-side down on serving tray. Repeat with remaining wrappers and salad. Use dressing as a dipping sauce.

Black and White Avocado Salad

PAREVE I GLUTEN-FREE I YIELDS 4-6 SERVINGS

INGREDIENTS

2-3 ripe Hass avocados

kosher salt
to taste

black pepper
to taste

1 Tbsp white sesame seeds

1 Tbsp black sesame seeds

pinch chili flakes

½ cup dried crunchy
chickpeas
(homemade or store-bought)

1 Tbsp extra light olive oil

juice of ½ lemon

METHOD

1   Shortly before serving, peel
    and pit avocados. Cut them
    into medium chunks. Place
    into a serving bowl.

2   Sprinkle with salt, pepper,
    sesame seeds, and chili
    flakes. Sprinkle with
    chickpeas; drizzle with
    oil and lemon juice. Serve
    immediately.

VARIATION

AVOCADO LETTUCE CUPS

Separate **radicchio** or **Boston lettuce leaves** to create individual lettuce cups. Follow recipe as directed, spooning about ⅓-cup avocado salad into each lettuce cup to plate as a pretty appetizer.

Shredded Kale and Brussels Sprouts Salad

PAREVE I GLUTEN-FREE I YIELDS 6-8 SERVINGS

INGREDIENTS

4 cups shredded kale

4 cups shredded
Brussels sprouts

3 scallions
sliced

½ cup raisins or dried
cranberries

½ cup toasted almonds

DRESSING

½ cup extra light olive oil

1 tsp lemon zest

juice of 2 lemons
(6-8 Tbsp)

2 Tbsp Dijon mustard

8 cloves garlic
minced (about 4 tsp)

2 tsp honey

½ small red onion
minced

METHOD

1   Place shredded kale into a
large bowl. Add Brussels
sprouts, scallions, and
raisins. Cover; refrigerate.

2   Dressing: Combine dressing
ingredients in a glass jar;
seal tightly and shake well.
Refrigerate.

3   Shortly before serving, toss
salad together with almonds
and dressing.

VARIATION

TEACUP SALAD

Prepare recipe as directed. Shortly before serving, plate salad in teacups or any type of unique cup.

Pretty to serve as an appetizer or at a party.

Baby Romaine Halves
With Lemon Dressing

PAREVE I GLUTEN-FREE I YIELDS 6-8 SERVINGS

INGREDIENTS

6 heads miniature romaine
bottom trimmed, halved

DRESSING

⅓ cup extra light olive oil

⅓ cup lemon juice
preferably fresh

1 tsp garlic powder

1 tsp kosher salt

black pepper

METHOD

1   Arrange miniature romaine halves in a single layer on a large serving platter.

2   Dressing: Combine dressing ingredients in a glass jar; seal tightly and shake well. Refrigerate.

3   Shortly before serving, drizzle dressing over romaine.

VARIATION

BBQ ROMAINE SALAD

Cut miniature romaine as directed. Coat a grill pan or barbecue grill with nonstick cooking spray. Grill romaine for 2-3 minutes per side. Transfer to a serving platter. Drizzle with dressing; top with ½ cup **pomegranate seeds** and ½ cup **toasted almonds** or any toppings of your choice.

Pretty Brussels Sprouts Salad

PAREVE I PASSOVER I GLUTEN-FREE I YIELDS 6-8 SERVINGS

INGREDIENTS

6-8 cups Brussels sprouts

2 cups celery
thinly sliced

3 scallions
thinly sliced

1 cup pomegranate seeds

¾ cup chopped candied
cashews or pecans

DRESSING

½ cup extra light olive oil

⅓ cup red wine vinegar

3 cloves garlic
minced (about 1½ tsp)

2 Tbsp honey

1½ tsp kosher salt

black pepper

3 Tbsp chopped fresh mint

METHOD

1   Using a serrated knife, trim
the root ends of the Brussels
sprouts so the leaves are
separated. Place leaves into
a large bowl. Add celery,
scallions and pomegranate
seeds. Cover; refrigerate

2 Dressing: Combine dressing ingredients in a glass jar; seal tightly and shake well. Refrigerate.

3 Before serving, toss salad with cashews and dressing.

VARIATION

QUINOA BRUSSELS SPROUTS SALAD

Cook 1 cup **quinoa** (see page 53) and add to salad.

Great for lunch the next day.

Rainbow Bright Salad

PAREVE I GLUTEN-FREE I YIELDS 6-8 SERVINGS

INGREDIENTS

4 cups romaine, arugula, or spinach leaves

1 cup shaved fresh corn (or frozen) kernels or diced mango

½ cup chopped red bell pepper or sliced cherry tomatoes

½ cup shredded carrots, diced orange bell pepper, or sliced oranges

1 cup sliced cucumbers, celery, or diced avocado

1 cup thinly sliced purple cabbage, or blueberries

⅓ cup dried cranberries

½ cup candied almonds, pecans, or cashews

DRESSING

⅓ cup extra light olive oil

2 Tbsp balsamic vinegar

1 Tbsp Dijon mustard

1 Tbsp pure maple syrup

2 cloves garlic minced (about 1 tsp)

1 tsp minced fresh thyme leaves

kosher salt

black pepper

METHOD

1 Place lettuce into a large serving bowl. Add toppings of your choice. Cover; refrigerate.

2 Dressing: Combine dressing ingredients in a glass jar; seal tightly and shake well. Refrigerate.

3 Shortly before serving, toss salad with dressing.

VARIATION

RAINBOW SALAD BOWLS

Place ½ cup lettuce into each individual bowl. Arrange toppings in a rainbow pattern. Drizzle with dressing before serving.

Baked Mini Falafel Ball Salad

PAREVE I GLUTEN-FREE OPTION I YIELDS 8-10 SERVINGS

INGREDIENTS

2 cups canned chickpeas
rinsed and drained

4 cloves garlic
(about 2 tsp)

½ cup chopped fresh parsley

3 Tbsp panko crumbs
(gluten-free or regular)

2 eggs

1 tsp kosher salt

black pepper

¼ tsp ground cumin

¼ tsp baking powder

1-2 Tbsp light olive oil
for brushing

8 cups arugula, kale,
or spring mix

1 ripe avocado

DRESSING

⅓ cup extra light olive oil

¼ cup tahini

2 Tbsp rice vinegar

1 clove garlic
minced (about ½ tsp)

3 Tbsp pure maple syrup

kosher salt

black pepper

METHOD

1   Falafel balls: Preheat oven to 400°F. Line a rimmed baking sheet with parchment paper.

2   Using a food processor fitted with the "S" blade, combine chickpeas, garlic, parsley, panko crumbs, eggs, salt, pepper, cumin, and baking powder.

3   Form mixture into small balls; arrange in a single layer on prepared baking sheet. Brush with oil. Bake for 20-25 minutes, or until lightly browned.

4   Dressing: Combine dressing ingredients in a glass jar; seal tightly and shake well.

5   Salad: Place salad greens into a large salad bowl. Shortly before serving, dice avocado; add to salad. Top with falafel balls. Drizzle with dressing.

VARIATION

KALE FALAFELS

Prepare recipe as directed. Place falafel balls, dressed greens, and diced avocado into large or small **pita breads.**

Three-Toned Cabbage Salad

PAREVE I GLUTEN-FREE I YIELDS 8-10 SERVINGS

INGREDIENTS

4 cups thinly sliced Napa
cabbage

4 cups thinly sliced bok choy

1 bag (16 oz/500 g) shredded
red cabbage

2 cups snow peas
*trimmed and cut into
1-inch pieces*

3 scallions
thinly sliced

¾ cup toasted slivered
almonds or pumpkin seeds

DRESSING

½ cup extra light olive oil

¼ cup rice vinegar

⅓ cup soy sauce or tamari

3 Tbsp honey

1½ tsp kosher salt
or to taste

½ tsp black pepper

1 tsp garlic powder

2 Tbsp white sesame seeds

2 Tbsp black sesame seeds

METHOD

1   In a large bowl, toss together Napa cabbage, bok choy, red cabbage, snow peas, and scallions. Cover; refrigerate.

2   Dressing: Combine dressing ingredients in a glass jar; seal tightly and shake well. Refrigerate.

3   Shortly before serving, add almonds and dressing; toss to combine.

VARIATION

INDIVIDUAL COLORED SALAD

Instead of combining all three cabbages, choose your favorite and create the salad with 9 cups of that cabbage. Works great and still tastes delicious. Alternatively, create a trio of salads, using the same dressing and the quantity listed for each cabbage.

Hemp Heart Cucumber Salad

PAREVE I GLUTEN-FREE I YIELDS 4-6 SERVINGS

INGREDIENTS

2 firm ripe tomatoes
diced

6 baby cucumbers
trimmed and cut into rounds

¼ cup diced red onion

**⅓ cup finely chopped
fresh parsley**

**⅓ cup finely chopped
fresh mint**

¼ cup hemp hearts

DRESSING

¼ cup extra light olive oil

3 Tbsp fresh lemon juice

1 clove garlic
minced (about ½ tsp)

¾ tsp kosher salt

black pepper

METHOD

1   In a large bowl, toss together tomatoes, cucumbers, red onion, parsley, and mint. Cover; refrigerate.

2   Dressing: Combine dressing ingredients In a glass jar; seal tightly and shake well. Refrigerate.

3   Before serving, toss salad with hemp hearts and dressing.

VARIATION

HEMP CUCUMBER CUPS

Prepare salad as directed, but finely dice the vegetables. Cut 2 long **cucumbers** into 2-inch chunks. Form cups by scooping out the seeds, being careful not to cut completely though. Fill each cucumber cup with 2-3 teapoons salad. Serve on individual plates.

High-Fiber Salad Topper

PAREVE I GLUTEN-FREE OPTION I FREEZES WELL I YIELDS ABOUT 5 CUPS

INGREDIENTS

1½ cups rolled oats
(gluten-free or regular)

½ cup slivered almonds
or other nuts

½ cup sunflower seeds
or pumpkin seeds

½ cup unsweetened
coconut flakes

½ cup chia seeds

¼ cup hemp hearts

2 tsp ground flax

2 Tbsp coconut oil

½ tsp ground cinnamon

pinch salt

1 tsp pure vanilla extract

2-3 Tbsp honey
or pure maple syrup

METHOD

1   Preheat oven to 325°F. Line
a large rimmed baking sheet
with parchment paper.

2   In a medium bowl, combine
all ingredients; mix well.

3   Spread oat mixture evenly
on prepared baking sheet.
Bake, uncovered, for 15-
20 minutes or until lightly
golden.

4   Let cool completely. Break into small, irregular
    pieces. Sprinkle over any salad.

5   Store in an airtight container. Topper will stay fresh
    for 1 week at room temperature.

VARIATION

FIBER TOPPER/SNACK

Prepare recipe as directed. Use as a
crunchy granola over **yogurt**, **rice**,
quinoa, or **fruit**. Makes a great snack
as well.

FISH

Hawaiian Poke Bowl

PAREVE I GLUTEN-FREE I YIELDS 4 BOWLS

INGREDIENTS

6 oz sushi grade
salmon or tuna
cubed

⅓ cup soy sauce or tamari

2 Tbsp toasted sesame oil

4 cloves garlic
minced (about 2 tsp)

2 tsp minced fresh ginger

2 cups cooked white or
brown rice

1 cup pineapple or
mango cubes

2 baby cucumbers
sliced

1 avocado

¼ cup chopped fresh
parsley or cilantro

white and black
sesame seeds
for garnish

chopped seaweed
for garnish

METHOD

1   In a large bowl, combine
    fish cubes with soy sauce,
    sesame oil, garlic, and ginger.
    Marinate for 20-30 minutes.

2   Arrange cooked rice, salmon
    (reserving marinade),
    pineapple, and cucumbers
    attractively in individual
    serving bowls.

3   Shortly before serving, peel, pit, and dice avocado. Add to serving bowls; top with parsley. Garnish with sesame seeds and seaweed. Drizzle with reserved marinade.

VARIATION

BAKED SALMON/TUNA BOWL

Prepare the marinade by combining soy sauce, sesame oil, garlic, and ginger. Coat a 9 x 13-inch baking dish with cooking spray. Add fish cubes; marinate 20-30 minutes.

Preheat oven to 375°F. Bake, uncovered, for 10-12 minutes. Serve as directed in Step 3.

Honey Mustard Pretzel Bites

PAREVE | GLUTEN-FREE OPTION | YIELD 4-6 SERVINGS

INGREDIENTS

4-6 individual salmon fillets
(about 6 oz/180 g each)

⅓ cup grainy Dijon mustard

2 Tbsp Dijon mustard

2 Tbsp extra light olive oil

2 Tbsp honey

2 cloves garlic
minced (about 1 tsp)

8-24 small pretzels
(gluten-free or regular)

METHOD

1   Preheat oven to 350°F. Line
a rimmed baking sheet with
parchment paper.

2   Cut fish into 2-inch chunks;
place onto prepared baking
sheet.

3   In a medium bowl, combine mustards with oil, honey, and garlic.

4   Spread 1-2 teaspoons mustard mixture onto top of each piece of fish. Top with a pretzel.

5   Bake, uncovered, for 12-15 minutes, or until salmon flakes easily when pierced with a fork. Serve hot or at room temperature.

VARIATION

PRETZEL SALMON

Prepare recipe as above, using 1 skinless, boneless **side of salmon** (about 2 lb/1 kg). After spreading mustard mixture on salmon, top with pretzels crushed into large crumbs.

Bake, uncovered, for 12-18 minutes.

French Fried Onion Salmon

PAREVE I FREEZES WELL I YIELDS 6 SERVINGS

INGREDIENTS

1 skinless, boneless side of salmon or 6 individual fillets
(about 2 lb/1 kg total)

kosher salt

black pepper

1½ cups French fried onions

¼ cup chopped fresh dill

1 Tbsp extra light olive oil

2 cloves garlic
minced (about 1 tsp)

2 3 Tbsp honey

METHOD

1   Preheat oven to 350°F. Line a large rimmed baking sheet with parchment paper.

2   Place salmon onto prepared baking sheet. Sprinkle generously with salt and pepper.

3 In a medium bowl, stir together onions, dill, oil, garlic, and honey. Spread mixture evenly over salmon.

4 Bake, uncovered, for 12-18 minutes, or until salmon flakes easily when pierced with a fork. Serve hot or at room temperature.

VARIATION

SALMON BAGELS

Prepare recipe as directed. Slice open 6-8 **bagels**; spread with **cream cheese**. Top with chunks of salmon.

Great for brunch.

Lemon Herbed Salmon Rolls With Asparagus

PAREVE I PASSOVER I GLUTEN-FREE I FREEZES WELL I YIELDS 4-6 SERVINGS

INGREDIENTS

4-6 individual salmon fillets
(about 6 oz/180 g each)

1-2 bunches asparagus
trimmed

3 Tbsp extra light olive oil

zest and juice of 2 lemons

¼ cup chopped fresh herbs
(dill, parsley, or mint)

1½ tsp kosher salt
or to taste

¼ tsp black pepper

METHOD

1   Preheat oven to 375°F. Line
    a rimmed baking sheet with
    parchment paper.

2   Cut each fillet lengthwise to
    form two thin long pieces.
    Place into large bowl. Add
    asparagus.

3   Add oil, lemon zest and juice,
    herbs, salt, and pepper; toss
    to coat fish and asparagus
    on all sides. Marinate for 10
    minutes.

4   Beginning from the thinner side of the
    salmon, roll it around the middle of 2 stalks
    of asparagus; place bundle on prepared
    baking sheet, seam-side down. Drizzle with
    remaining marinade.

5   Bake, uncovered, for 12-15 minutes, or until
    salmon flakes when pierced with a fork. Serve
    hot or at room temperature.

VARIATION

SALMON "SUSHI"

Cut each asparagus spear into 3-4-
inch pieces. Prepare fish as directed;
wrap each slice of salmon around
each asparagus piece to look like
sushi.

Pretty Pomegranate Salmon

PAREVE I GLUTEN-FREE I YIELDS 6 SERVINGS

INGREDIENTS

1 skinless, boneless side of
salmon or arctic char
(2 lb/1 kg) or 4-6 individual fillets

kosher salt

black pepper

TOPPING

½ cup tahini sauce
(store-bought or homemade)

¼ cup chopped flat leaf
parsley

¾ cup pomegranate seeds

METHOD

1   Preheat oven to 425°F. Line
a large rimmed baking sheet
with parchment paper.

2   Place salmon on prepared
baking sheet. Sprinkle
generously with salt and
pepper.

3   Bake, uncovered, for 15-18 minutes, or until
    salmon flakes when lightly pierced with a fork.
    When cool, transfer to a serving platter.

4   Shortly before serving, spread salmon with a
    layer of tahini sauce.

5   Sprinkle with parsley. Scatter on pomegranate
    seeds. Using your hand, lightly press down on
    topping to adhere it.

VARIATION

FIG SALMON

Prepare recipe as directed, using
8-10 **fresh figs**, quartered, in place of
pomegranate seeds.

"Smashed" Salmon

PAREVE I PASSOVER I GLUTEN-FREE I FREEZES WELL I YIELDS 4-6 SERVINGS

INGREDIENTS

4-6 individual salmon fillets
(about 6 oz/180 g each)

extra light olive oil

kosher salt

black pepper

METHOD

1   Preheat broiler. Line a
    rimmed baking sheet with
    aluminum foil; coat with
    nonstick cooking spray.

2   Place fish in a single layer on prepared baking sheet. Using the prongs of a fork, smash salmon to flatten it, but try not to cut all the way through.

3   Using a silicone brush, brush salmon lightly with oil. Sprinkle generously with salt and pepper.

4   Broil for 8-10 minutes (no turning required), until fish becomes crunchy and golden. Sprinkle with additional salt.

VARIATION

SALMON SALAD

Follow recipe as directed. Cut broiled salmon into 2-3 pieces; plate on a simple **garden salad**, **Simply Sweet Mini Pepper Salad** (p. 62) or **Shredded Kale and Brussels Sprouts Salad** (p. 74).

Serve as an appetizer or as a great brunch option.

Black Sesame-Crusted Fish

PAREVE I GLUTEN-FREE OPTION I FREEZES WELL I YIELDS 4-6 SERVINGS

INGREDIENTS

4-6 white fish fillets
(about 6 oz/180 g each)
(e.g., halibut, tilapia, turbot,
pickerel, or sole)

1½ tsp kosher salt

¼ tsp black pepper

1½ tsp sweet paprika

**1¼ cups unseasoned
panko crumbs**
(gluten-free or regular)

**3-4 Tbsp black
sesame seeds**

2 Tbsp extra light olive oil

METHOD

1   Preheat oven to 400°F. Line
a rimmed baking sheet with
parchment paper.

2   Place fish in a single layer on prepared baking sheet.

3   In a medium bowl, combine salt, pepper, paprika, panko crumbs, sesame seeds, and oil; mix well. Sprinkle generously over fish.

4   Bake, uncovered, for 12-15 minutes, or until fish flakes easily when pierced with a fork.

VARIATION

FISH TACOS

Prepare recipe as directed. Wrap fish in **tortilla wraps**. Add **fresh veggies** and **coleslaw**; drizzle with **lime juice**.

Salmon With 3 Spice Rubs

PAREVE | GLUTEN-FREE | FREEZES WELL | YIELDS 4-6 SERVINGS

INGREDIENTS

4-6 salmon fillets
(about 6 oz/180 g each)

SESAME SPICE RUB

2 Tbsp sweet paprika

2 tsp dried oregano

2 tsp ground cumin

4 Tbsp white sesame seeds

2 tsp kosher salt

1-2 Tbsp extra light olive oil

3-4 Tbsp honey
for drizzling

HERB SPICE RUB

2 tsp kosher salt

2 Tbsp dried parsley

2 Tbsp dried basil

pinch chili flakes

3 Tbsp onion powder

1-2 Tbsp extra light olive oil

3-4 Tbsp honey
for drizzling

GARLIC SPICE RUB

2 tsp sweet paprika

1 Tbsp brown sugar

2 tsp garlic powder

2 tsp onion powder

1 tsp kosher salt

1 tsp black pepper

1-2 Tbsp extra light olive oil

2-3 Tbsp honey
for drizzling

METHOD

1   Preheat oven to 375°F. Line a large rimmed baking sheet with parchment paper.

2   Arrange salmon in a single layer on prepared baking sheet.

3   In a medium bowl, combine spices for the spice rub of your choice; mix well.

4   Spread mixture evenly over salmon. Drizzle with oil and honey.

5   Bake, uncovered, for 12-15 minutes, or until salmon flakes easily when pierced with a fork. Serve hot or at room temperature.

VARIATION

SPICED RUBS

These spice rubs can also be used on other types of fish and as a rub for meat roasts.

No-Mayo Avocado Tuna Salad

PAREVE I GLUTEN-FREE I YIELDS 4-6 SERVINGS

INGREDIENTS

2 cans white tuna
(6 oz/170 g each)
well drained and flaked

1 baby cucumber
trimmed and cut into rounds

⅓ cup diced red onion

¼ cup fresh herbs
(e.g., basil, mint, cilantro)

2 firm Hass avocados

2 Tbsp fresh lemon juice

2 Tbsp extra light olive oil

1 tsp kosher salt

black pepper

METHOD

1   In a large bowl, combine
    tuna with cucumber rounds,
    red onion, and fresh herbs.
    Cover; refrigerate.

2   Shortly before serving, peel,
    pit, and dice avocados. Add
    to tuna mixture.

3   Drizzle with lemon juice
    and oil; sprinkle with salt
    and pepper. Toss gently to
    combine. Serve immediately.

VARIATION

TUNA NACHOS

Prepare recipe as directed. Place
nacho chips onto a serving platter or
bowl; top with tuna mixture. Serve as
an appetizer.

Crispy "Popcorn" Fish Bites

PAREVE I GLUTEN-FREE OPTION I FREEZES WELL I YIELDS 6 SERVINGS

INGREDIENTS

4-6 white fish fillets
(about 6 oz/180 g each)
(e.g., halibut, tilapia, turbot,
pickerel, or sole)

1¼ cups flour
(or gluten-free flour)

1 Tbsp onion powder

1 Tbsp sweet paprika

¼ tsp black pepper

1 tsp kosher salt

2 eggs

oil
for frying

SAUCE

⅓ cup ketchup

2 Tbsp honey

2 Tbsp soy sauce or tamari

2 Tbsp fresh lemon juice

METHOD

1   Cut fish fillets into bite-size
    pieces.

2   In a medium bowl, combine
    flour, onion powder, paprika,
    pepper, and salt; mix well.
    Lightly beat eggs in a second
    bowl.

VARIATION

FRIED FISH FILLETS

Instead of cutting the fish into bite-size pieces, use the whole fillets. Prepare recipe as directed.

3   Dip fish first into eggs, then into flour mixture, coating all sides.

4   In a large nonstick skillet, heat oil over medium-high heat. Working in batches, fry fish on all sides until golden, crispy, and cooked through, 3-5 minutes. Transfer to a platter; pat with a paper towel to remove excess oil.

5   Sauce: In a small bowl, combine ketchup, honey, soy sauce, and lemon juice. Drizzle sauce over fish or serve it on the side.

Lemon Dill Fish

PAREVE | PASSOVER | GLUTEN-FREE | FREEZES WELL | YIELDS 4-6 SERVINGS

INGREDIENTS

4-6 white fish fillets
(about 6 oz/180 g each)
(e.g., halibut, tilapia, turbot,
pickerel, or sole)

1 medium bunch fresh dill
chopped

1 tsp kosher salt

black pepper

2 cloves garlic
minced (about 1 tsp)

1 Tbsp fresh lemon zest

juice of ½ lemon
(preferably fresh)

2 Tbsp extra light olive oil

METHOD

1   Preheat oven to 400°F. Line
a rimmed baking sheet with
parchment paper.

2   Arrange fish in a single layer
on prepared baking sheet

3   Scatter dill over fish. Sprinkle with salt, pepper, garlic, and zest. Drizzle with lemon juice and oil.

4   Bake, uncovered, for 12-15 minutes, or until fish flakes with a fork and dill is toasted.

VARIATION

PEPPER DILL FISH

Cut 2 **bell peppers** (any colors) into rounds. Place onto prepared baking sheet along with fish; prepare recipe as directed.

Seared Sriracha Honey Salmon

PAREVE I GLUTEN-FREE I FREEZES WELL I YIELDS 4-6 SERVINGS

INGREDIENTS

4-6 large salmon fillets
(about 6 oz/180 g each)

2 Tbsp rice vinegar

2 Tbsp soy sauce or tamari

3-4 tsp sriracha sauce
or to taste

2 Tbsp honey

2 cloves garlic
minced (about 1 tsp)

1 tsp kosher salt
or to taste

2 Tbsp toasted sesame oil
for frying

2 Tbsp toasted white
sesame seeds
for garnish

METHOD

1   Place salmon fillets, vinegar, soy sauce,
    sriracha, honey, garlic, and salt into a large
    resealable plastic bag. Seal tightly; marinate
    for 20-30 minutes.

2   In a large skillet, heat sesame oil over
    medium-high heat. Remove fish from
    marinade; discard marinade.

3   Sear salmon fillets about 4 minutes per side,
    until golden. When done, fish will flake when
    pressed gently with a fork. Sprinkle with
    sesame seeds.

VARIATION

TOPPED SRIRACHA SALMON

Prepare recipe as directed. Shortly
before serving, trim the ends of a
large **tomato**; slice thinly. Place slices
on prepared fish. Peel, pit, and slice
1-2 avocados; place on tomato slices.
Serve.

CHICKEN

Sweet Granola Chicken

MEAT I GLUTEN-FREE OPTION I FREEZES WELL I YIELDS 6 SERVINGS

INGREDIENTS

6 skinless, boneless
chicken cutlets
white or dark, pounded thin

½ cup apricot jam

1 cup large flake rolled oats
(gluten-free or regular)

½ cup panko crumbs
(gluten-free or regular)

⅓ cup slivered
or sliced almonds
(optional)

1 tsp ground cinnamon

2 Tbsp pure maple syrup

pinch kosher salt

3-4 Tbsp extra light olive oil

METHOD

1   Preheat oven to 400°F. Line
    a large rimmed baking sheet
    with parchment paper.

2   Arrange chicken in a single
    layer on prepared baking
    sheet. Spread apricot jam
    evenly over chicken.

3   In a medium bowl, combine oats with panko, almonds (if using), cinnamon, maple syrup, salt, and oil; mix well.

4   Spread oat mixture evenly over top of chicken.

5   Bake, uncovered, for 25-30 minutes, or until cooked through and juices run clear. Cooking time will depend on thickness of chicken.

VARIATION

GRANOLA CHICKEN TENDERS

Cut chicken into long thin strips. Prepare recipe as directed. Bake, uncovered, for 20-25 minutes, until cooked through. Serve with **ketchup** or any **dipping sauce**.

Sheet Pan Chicken With Heirloom Carrots and Sweet Potatoes

MEAT I PASSOVER I GLUTEN-FREE I FREEZES WELL I YIELDS 6 SERVINGS

INGREDIENTS

1 whole chicken *(about 3 lb/1.4 kg)*
cut into eighths

1-2 large sweet potatoes
trimmed and cut into rounds (do not peel)

4-6 heirloom or regular carrots

1½ tsp kosher salt
or to taste

black pepper

1 Tbsp garlic powder

1 Tbsp sweet paprika

2 Tbsp extra light olive oil

¼ cup honey or silan

¼ cup chopped fresh parsley
plus additional for garnish

METHOD

1   Preheat oven to 375°F. Line a large rimmed baking sheet with parchment paper.

2   Trim and discard excess fat from chicken. Place chicken and potatoes in a single layer on prepared baking sheet.

3   Trim and peel carrots. Cut each in half crosswise, then lengthwise into 4 pieces. Scatter onto baking sheet.

4   Sprinkle chicken and vegetables with salt, pepper, garlic powder, and paprika. Drizzle with oil, honey, and parsley, coating all sides.

5   Roast, uncovered, for about 1 hour, or until chicken, potatoes, and carrots are glazed and golden. Garnish with additional parsley.

SHREDDED CHICKEN BOWL

Prepare recipe as directed. Once chicken is cooked through, discard skin and pull chicken with two forks, creating shredded chicken. Place into a bowl; top with carrots and sweet potatoes for a full meal in one bowl. Alternatively, prepare this recipe using skinless, boneless chicken (white or dark); reduce baking time to 35-45 minutes.

Kale Chicken

MEAT I GLUTEN-FREE I CHICKEN FREEZES WELL I YIELDS 4-6 SERVINGS

INGREDIENTS

1 whole chicken
(about 3 lb/1.4 kg)
cut into eighths

kosher salt

black pepper

1 Tbsp garlic powder

juice of 1 lemon

4 Tbsp extra light olive oil
divided

2 Tbsp black sesame seeds

1 medium bunch kale
(about 1 lb/500 g)

METHOD

1   Preheat oven to 400°F. Line
    a rimmed baking sheet with
    parchment paper.

2   Trim and discard excess fat
    from chicken. Arrange in a
    single layer, skin-side up,
    on prepared baking sheet.
    Season generously with salt,
    pepper, and garlic powder.
    Drizzle with lemon juice and
    2 tablespoons oil; sprinkle
    with sesame seeds.

3   Bake, uncovered, for 45 minutes.

4   Meanwhile, wash kale thoroughly; pat dry.
     Remove and discard tough stalks and center
     veins. Tear kale into large pieces. Place into
     large bowl. Toss with remaining 2 tablespoons
     olive oil; sprinkle with salt and pepper.

5   Remove chicken from oven. Place kale around
     chicken. Return to oven; bake, 10-15 minutes
     longer, until chicken juices run clear and kale is
     crunchy.

VARIATION

KALE-STUFFED CHICKEN

Cut slits into **6 skinless, boneless
chicken cutlets** (white or dark),
being careful not to cut fully through.
Stuff slits with kale that has been
dressed with oil, salt, and pepper (see
recipe). Season chicken as directed.
Bake, uncovered, for 35-40 minutes,
depending on thickness of chicken.

Old-Fashioned BBQ Chicken

MEAT I GLUTEN-FREE I FREEZES WELL I YIELDS 4-6 SERVINGS

INGREDIENTS

1 whole chicken
(about 3 lb /1.4 kg)
cut into eighths

2 tsp garlic powder

2 tsp onion powder

2 tsp sweet paprika

1 tsp ground ginger

1 tsp kosher salt

¼ tsp black pepper

2-3 Tbsp extra light olive oil

1 cup barbeque sauce

METHOD

1   Preheat oven to 375°F. Line
a rimmed baking sheet with
foil; coat with nonstick cooking
spray. Trim and discard excess
fat from chicken.

2   Arrange chicken in a single
layer on prepared baking
sheet.

3   Sprinkle with garlic powder,
onion powder, paprika,
ginger, salt, and pepper,
coating all sides. Drizzle
with oil.

VARIATION

4   Bake, uncovered, for about 40 minutes.

5   Remove from oven; using a silicone brush, brush barbecue sauce over chicken. Repeat until all the sauce has been used.

6   Preheat broiler; broil chicken, uncovered, for 3-5 minutes, until skin is crunchy. (Check on chicken often as it broils so it doesn't burn).

BBQ DRUMSTICKS

Prepare recipe as directed, using **12 drumsticks**. Serve to kids with a side of boiled **corn on the cob**.

Lemon Rosemary Chicken

MEAT | PASSOVER | GLUTEN-FREE | FREEZES WELL | YIELDS 6 SERVINGS

INGREDIENTS

6 skinless, boneless
chicken cutlets
white or dark

3 Tbsp extra light olive oil

1½ Tbsp minced fresh
rosemary

2 Tbsp lemon zest
(from about 4 lemons)

2 Tbsp lemon juice
(preferably fresh)

6 cloves garlic
minced (about 2 Tbsp)

2 tsp kosher salt

black pepper, *to taste*

1 lemon
trimmed and sliced

METHOD

1   Preheat oven to 400°F. Line
    a rimmed baking sheet with
    parchment paper.

2   Arrange chicken in a single
    layer on prepared baking
    sheet.

3   In a small bowl combine oil,
    rosemary, lemon zest, lemon
    juice, garlic, salt, and pepper;
    mix well.

4   Spoon over chicken, coating all sides. Arrange lemon slices around chicken.

5   Bake, uncovered, for 30-35 minutes, or until cooked through and juices run clear. Cooking time will depend on thickness of chicken.

VARIATION

BBQ CHICKEN SKEWERS

Soak 12-15 bamboo skewers in water for 10 minutes. Cut chicken into 1-inch chunks. Place into a bowl; add remaining ingredients; mix well. Thread chicken onto skewers.

Preheat grill. Grill over indirect heat for 4-5 minutes per side, until grill marks appear and juices run clear. Serve on individual plates as an appetizer or as the main course.

Salami Hasselback Chicken

MEAT I GLUTEN-FREE I FREEZES WELL I YIELDS 4-6 SERVINGS

INGREDIENTS

6 single skinless, boneless
chicken breasts

1 beef salami
(1 lb/.5 kg) thinly sliced

½ cup ketchup

2 Tbsp apple cider vinegar

3 Tbsp honey

2 Tbsp soy sauce or tamari

2 cloves garlic
minced (about 1 tsp)

pinch chili flakes

METHOD

1 Preheat oven to 400°F. Coat
   a 9 x 13-inch baking dish
   with nonstick cooking spray.

2 Using a serrated knife,
   carefully cut 3-4 slits into
   each chicken breast, not
   cutting all the way through.
   Carefully arrange breasts in a
   single layer in prepared dish.

3 Cut each slice of salami in
   half, forming half-moons.
   Tuck 1-2 half-moons into
   each slit.

4   In a medium bowl, stir together ketchup, vinegar, honey, soy sauce, garlic, and chili flakes.

5   Pour on sauce to coat chicken and salami on all sides. Push chicken pieces together so that salami is securely in place.

6   Bake, uncovered, for 30-35 minutes, depending on the thickness of the chicken, until juices run clear.

VARIATION

SALAMI CHICKEN BITES

Cut chicken into 2-inch pieces; place into a medium bowl. Add salami "moons" and remaining ingredients; mix well. Arrange in a single layer on a parchment-lined baking sheet. Bake, uncovered, for 15-20 minutes, until chicken is golden. Using toothpicks, pierce chunks of chicken and salami; place onto a serving platter. Serve family style, on individual plates, or as an appetizer for a party.

Rustic Sheet Pan Chicken

MEAT I GLUTEN-FREE I FREEZES WELL I YIELDS 4-6 SERVINGS

INGREDIENTS

1 whole chicken
(about 3 lb/ 1.4 kg) cut into
eighths

4 medium carrots
trimmed, peeled, and cut in half
crosswise and then lengthwise

1 can (19 oz/540 ml)
chickpeas
rinsed and drained

1 cup dried fruit
(e.g., raisins, apricots, prunes)

1 tsp kosher salt

¼ tsp black pepper

2 tsp onion powder

2 tsp garlic powder

3 Tbsp sweet paprika

2 Tbsp extra light olive oil

3 Tbsp pure maple syrup
or honey

METHOD

1   Preheat oven to 375°F. Line
a large rimmed baking sheet
with parchment paper.

2   Trim and discard excess
fat from chicken. Arrange
chicken, skin-side up, in a
single layer on prepared
baking sheet.

3   Scatter carrots, chickpeas, and dried fruit
around chicken. Sprinkle with salt, pepper,
onion powder, garlic powder, and paprika.
Drizzle with oil and maple syrup; toss to coat.

4   Bake, uncovered, for 50-60 minutes, or until
chicken juices run clear when pierced with a
fork.

VARIATION

RUSTIC COUSCOUS

Meatless main: Omit chicken. Cook
1½ cups couscous according to
package directions. Meanwhile,
toss carrots, chickpeas, and dried
fruit on prepared baking sheet
with spices,oil, and maple syrup as
directed in Step 3. Bake, uncovered,
at 375°F for 40 minutes or until
golden. Place couscous onto a large
serving platter; top with roasted
veggies and dried fruit.

Glazed Grilled Chicken

MEAT I PASSOVER I GLUTEN-FREE I FREEZES WELL I YIELDS 6 SERVINGS

INGREDIENTS

2 tsp sweet paprika

1 tsp chili powder

1 tsp cumin

1 tsp dried thyme or rosemary

1 tsp kosher salt

¼ tsp black pepper

1 tsp garlic powder

6 single skinless, boneless chicken cutlets
white or dark

2 Tbsp extra light olive oil

GLAZE

3 Tbsp red wine vinegar

2 Tbsp honey

METHOD

1   In a large bowl, combine paprika, chili powder, cumin, thyme, salt, pepper, and garlic powder; mix well. Add chicken; rub spices onto chicken to coat all sides.

2   Heat oil on a grill pan or in a nonstick skillet over medium-high heat. Working in batches, grill chicken 4-6 minutes per side, until grill marks appear and juices run clear.

3   Glaze: In a small bowl, mix together vinegar and honey. Using a silicone brush, lightly brush mixture over cooked chicken.

VARIATION

GRILLED CHICKEN SKEWERS

Cut red, yellow, and/or orange **bell peppers** into large cubes. Prepare recipe as directed. Cut grilled chicken into chunks; thread onto metal or wooden **skewers**, alternating with peppers. Alternatively, soak wooden skewers for 5-8 minutes. Preheat grill pan or barbecue grill. Cut uncooked chicken into chunks; thread chicken and peppers onto skewers. Grill on each side for 7-10 minutes, until cooked through.

Tomato Garlic Chicken

MEAT I GLUTEN-FREE I FREEZES WELL I YIELDS 4-6 SERVINGS

INGREDIENTS

1 chicken (about 3 lb/1.4 kg)
cut into eighths

2 cups halved cherry
tomatoes

1 tsp kosher salt

black pepper
to taste

1½ tsp sweet paprika

8 cloves garlic
minced (about 4 tsp)

2 Tbsp extra light olive oil

3 Tbsp red wine vinegar

2 Tbsp honey

¼ cup chopped fresh basil
plus more for garnish

METHOD

1   Preheat oven to 375°F. Coat
    a 9 x 13-inch baking dish
    with nonstick cooking spray.

2   Trim and discard excess fat
    from chicken pieces. Arrange
    chicken, skin-side up, in
    prepared dish.

3   Sprinkle generously with salt, pepper, paprika, and garlic. Drizzle with oil, vinegar, and honey; rub to coat on all sides. Top with basil. Add tomatoes, tucking them between pieces of chicken.

4   Roast, uncovered, for about 1 hour. When done, chicken juices run clear when chicken is pierced with a fork. Garnish with additional basil.

VARIATION

TOMATO CHICKEN TOPPER

Follow Step 1. Cut **6 skinless, boneless chicken cutlets** (white or dark) into 2-inch pieces. Place into prepared baking dish; add tomatoes. Continue with Step 3. Bake, uncovered, for 40 minutes, until juices run clear. Serve over cooked **quinoa**, **rice**, or **spaghetti**. Garnish with basil. Great for an easy dinner.

Baked Almond Flour Chicken

MEAT I PASSOVER I GLUTEN-FREE I FREEZES WELL I YIELDS 6 SERVINGS

INGREDIENTS

2 cups almond flour

2 tsp sweet paprika

¼ tsp black pepper

1½ tsp kosher salt

2 tsp garlic powder

3 Tbsp minced
chopped parsley

2 eggs

12 drumsticks or
1 whole chicken
(about 3 lb/1.4 kg)
cut into eighths

METHOD

1 Preheat oven to 375°F. Line
a large rimmed baking sheet
with parchment paper.

2 In a medium bowl, combine
almond flour, paprika,
pepper, salt, garlic powder,
parsley

3 In a second bowl, lightly beat
eggs.

4   Dip chicken pieces into egg mixture, then into almond mixture, coating all sides. Place onto prepared baking sheet.

5   Bake, uncovered, for 35-45 minutes for drumsticks or 1 hour for whole chicken, or until cooked through and juices run clear. Baking time will depend on thickness of chicken.

VARIATION

ALMOND FLOUR SCHNITZEL

Prepare recipe as directed. Use 6 pieces of **skinless, boneless chicken cutlets** (white or dark). Heat oil in a nonstick frying pan; fry each side 4-5 minutes, until cooked through and juices run clear. Top with parsley.

Honey-Glazed Sunflower Seed Chicken

PAREVE I GLUTEN FREE I FREEZES WELL I YIELDS 6 SERVINGS

INGREDIENTS

6 single skinless, boneless
chicken cutlets
white or dark

kosher salt

black pepper

1 cup shelled
sunflower seeds
(salted or unsalted)

⅓ cup chopped
flat leaf parsley

2 Tbsp extra light olive oil

3 Tbsp honey

METHOD

1   Preheat oven to 375°F. Line
a large rimmed baking sheet
with parchment paper.

2   Lightly sprinkle chicken on
both sides with salt and
pepper. Arrange in a single
layer on prepared baking
sheet.

3   In a medium bowl, combine sunflower seeds with parsley, oil, and honey; mix well.

4   Spread sunflower seed mixture evenly over tops of chicken.

5   Bake, uncovered, for 30-35 minutes, or until cooked through and juices run clear. Cooking time will depend on thickness of breasts.

VARIATION

PUMPKIN SEED CHICKEN

Follow recipe as directed, using 1 cup **pumpkin seeds**, salted or unsalted, in place of sunflower seeds.

Spaghetti Squash Chicken

MEAT I PASSOVER I GLUTEN-FREE I FREEZES WELL I YIELDS 4-6 SERVINGS

INGREDIENTS

1 medium spaghetti squash
(about 3 lb/1.4 kg)

1 whole chicken
(about 3 lb/1.4 kg) cut into
eighths

kosher salt

black pepper

1¼ cups marinara sauce

½ cup chopped fresh basil
divided

METHOD

1   Preheat oven to 375°F. Line
a 9 x 13-inch baking dish
with parchment paper.

2   Cut squash in half
lengthwise; discard seeds
and pulp. Place squash,
cut-side down, into
prepared baking dish.
Bake, uncovered, for 35-
45 minutes, until tender.
Remove parchment with
squash from baking dish.
Let cool.

3   Coat the same baking dish with nonstick cooking spray. Use a fork to separate squash strands; discard rind. Place strands into prepared baking dish; season with salt and pepper.

4   Trim and discard excess fat from chicken pieces. Arrange chicken in a single layer, skin-side up, over squash strands.

5   Sprinkle chicken with salt and pepper, then spoon marinara sauce over the top. Scatter with half the basil.

6   Bake, uncovered, for about 1 hour, until glazed and golden and juices run clear. Garnish with remaining basil.

VARIATION

CHICKEN IN SQUASH HALVES

Cut squash in half; discard seeds and pulp. Pour ½ cup marinara sauce into each squash cavity. Top with **skinless, boneless chicken cutlets** (about 6, white or dark) cut into 2-inch pieces, and sprinkle with parsley. Bake, uncovered, for 40-50 minutes.

Potato Latke Schnitzel

MEAT I PASSOVER I GLUTEN-FREE I FREEZES WELL I YIELDS 6 SERVINGS

INGREDIENTS

8 large Yukon potatoes

1 large onion
cut into chunks

2 eggs

¼ cup potato starch

1 tsp baking powder

1 tsp kosher salt

¼ tsp black pepper

6 single skinless,
boneless chicken cutlets
(white or dark) pounded thin

oil
for frying

ketchup, for serving

mustard, for serving

METHOD

1   In a food processor fitted
with the shredding disk,
shred potatoes and onion,
using medium pressure.
Transfer vegetables to a
large colander set in the
sink or over a bowl; press
firmly to drain excess liquid.

2   Place drained veggies into
a large bowl. Add eggs,
potato starch, baking
powder, salt, and pepper.
Mix well.

3   Place chicken into potato mixture; coat on all sides.

4   In a large nonstick skillet, heat oil over medium-high heat. Working in batches, fry chicken on both sides until cooked through and juices run clear, 3-5 minutes per side.

5   Pat chicken with paper towel to remove excess oil.

6   Serve with ketchup and mustard, as desired.

VARIATION

SWEET POTATO SCHNITZEL

Prepare recipe as directed using 3-4 large **sweet potatoes.**

Honey Mustard Chicken and Steak Dinner

MEAT I GLUTEN-FREE I FREEZES WELL I YIELDS 6 SERVINGS

INGREDIENTS

4 skinless, boneless chicken cutlets
(white or dark) cut into 1-inch strips

1 skirt steak (2 lb/1 kg)
cut into 1-inch strips

2 Tbsp grapeseed or vegetable oil

kosher salt
to taste

black pepper
to taste

2 cloves garlic
minced (about 1 tsp)

⅓ cup honey

⅓ cup soy sauce or tamari

¼ cup Dijon mustard

1 bunch chives
chopped

METHOD

1. In a large frying pan, heat oil over medium heat.

2. Add chicken and steak strips; sauté 6-8 minutes, until nicely browned.

3. Sprinkle with salt, pepper, and garlic. Stir in honey, soy sauce, and mustard. Cook 5-8 minutes, stirring occasionally, until sauce reduces to half.

4. Shortly before serving, sprinkle with chives.

VARIATION

RICE NOODLE DINNER

For a complete meal, serve Honey Mustard Chicken and Steak Dinner stirred into **rice noodles, couscous, quinoa,** or **pasta**.

MEAT

Skirt Steak Strips
With Tahini Herb Sauce

MEAT I GLUTEN-FREE I FREEZES WELL I YIELDS 4-6 SERVINGS

INGREDIENTS

TAHINI HERB SAUCE

½ cup fresh basil leaves
finely chopped

½ cup fresh parsley leaves
finely chopped

1 Tbsp honey

2 cloves garlic
minced (about 1 tsp)

3 Tbsp rice vinegar

2 Tbsp soy sauce or tamari

3 Tbsp tahini

2 Tbsp extra light olive oil

2 Tbsp lemon juice
(preferably fresh)

1 skirt steak, hanger steak,
or flank steak *(about 2 lb/1 kg)*

METHOD

1 In a small container or jar,
combine ingredients for
tahini sauce; shake well
(or use a food processor
or immersion blender to
combine). Refrigerate until
serving time.

2 Preheat oven to 375°F. Line
a rimmed baking sheet with
parchment paper.

3   Transfer meat to prepared baking sheet. Roast for 15-20 minutes or grill for 4-6 minutes per side until meat reaches desired doneness. (For medium, cook to 145°F.)

4   Let steak rest for 5 minutes. Slice against the grain, on the diagonal, into thin slices. Serve tahini herb sauce in a bowl or drizzle over meat.

VARIATION

SKIRT STEAK TAHINI SALAD

Prepare recipe as directed. Top a **garden salad** or **kale salad** with sliced steak. Shortly before serving, toss salad with tahini herb sauce.

This sauce can also be used over vegetables, quinoa, rice, etc.

Sesame-Crusted London Broil

MEAT I GLUTEN-FREE OPTION I FREEZES WELL I YIELDS 6 SERVINGS

INGREDIENTS

1 London broil
(about 2 lb/1 kg)

kosher salt
to taste

black pepper
to taste

⅓ cup soy sauce or tamari

3 Tbsp honey

2 Tbsp extra light olive oil

3 Tbsp white sesame seeds
toasted

METHOD

1   Sprinkle London broil lightly on both sides with salt and pepper and place into a resealable plastic bag. Add soy sauce, honey, and oil; seal bag tightly. Massage meat on both sides with marinade. Marinate for 1 hour or overnight In the refrigerator.

2   Coat a grill pan with nonstick cooking spray; heat over medium-high.

3   Remove London broil from marinade; discard marinade. Grill meat for 7-8 minutes per side or until meat reaches desired doneness. (For medium, cook meat to an internal temperature of 145°F.)

4   Place meat onto a cutting board; let rest for 5 minutes. Slice against the grain on the diagonal, into thin slices. Place onto serving platter. Sprinkle with toasted sesame seeds.

VARIATION

STEAK BITES

Prepare recipe as directed through Step 3. Cut each piece of meat into cubes. Using toothpicks, pierce each cube; sprinkle with sesame seeds. Serve family style, on individual plates, or as an appetizer for a party.

Bruschetta London Broil

MEAT I GLUTEN-FREE I FREEZES WELL I YIELDS 6 SERVINGS

INGREDIENTS

1 London broil (about 2 lb/ 1kg)

kosher salt

black pepper

1 Tbsp garlic powder

BRUSCHETTA TOPPING

2 Tbsp extra light olive oil

1 small red onion
diced

4 cloves garlic
minced (about 2 tsp)

4 medium tomatoes
trimmed and diced

⅓ cup chopped fresh basil

juice of 1 lemon

1 tsp kosher salt

black pepper

METHOD

1   Sprinkle London broil with salt, pepper, and garlic powder, coating all sides. Let sit for 20 minutes.

2   Bruschetta: Meanwhile, in a skillet, heat oil over medium-high heat. Add onion and garlic; sauté for 5-7 minutes or until onion is golden. Stir in tomatoes, basil, lemon juice, salt, and pepper. Cook for 3-5 minutes, until tomatoes have slightly broken down.

3   Meat: Coat a grill pan with nonstick cooking spray; heat over medium high heat. Add meat; grill for 7-8 minutes per side or until meat reaches desired doneness. (For medium, grill to an internal temperature of 145°F.)

4   Place meat onto a cutting board; let rest for 5 minutes. Slice against the grain, on the diagonal, into thin slices. Place onto a serving platter.

5   Pour bruschetta over sliced London broil and serve. Bruschetta can be served hot or at room temperature.

VARIATION

LONDON BROIL CROSTINI

Preheat oven to 400°F. Cut 1 large **baguette** into slices about 1-inch thick. Toast for 4-6 minutes, until golden. Prepare recipe as directed through Step 4. Place a meat slice onto the toasted bread; top with bruschetta. Serve on a platter.

Marinated Hot Pepper Brisket

MEAT I GLUTEN-FREE I FREEZES WELL I YIELDS 10-12 SERVINGS

INGREDIENTS

1 beef brisket
(about 5-6 lb/2.3-2.7 kg)

2 medium red onions
chopped

2 tsp kosher salt

black pepper

1 tsp garlic powder

2½ cups marinara sauce

1 cup marinated
sliced hot peppers
drained

¼ cup apple cider vinegar

½ cup soy sauce or tamari

¼ cup honey

½ cup chopped
fresh parsley
plus more for garnish

METHOD

1   Preheat oven to 325°F.
Place brisket and onions into
a large roasting pan coated
with nonstick cooking spray.
Sprinkle with salt, pepper,
and garlic powder. Rub to
coat on all sides.

2   Make a sauce by combining
marinara sauce, hot peppers,
vinegar, soy sauce, honey,
and parsley; mix well. Pour
sauce over, around, and
under brisket and onions.

3   Bake, covered, for 3½-4 hours, or until meat
    is fork-tender. Calculate 45 minutes per pound
    to determine the cooking time.

4   Let cool. Refrigerate for several hours or
    overnight.

5   Remove and discard hardened fat from gravy.
    Slice against the grain to desired thickness.

6   Reheat, covered, in pan gravy at 350°F for 25-
    30 minutes. Garnish with parsley.

VARIATION

SWEET POTATO BRISKET

Preheat oven to 400°F. Line a rimmed
baking sheet with parchment paper.
Cut 4-5 large **sweet potatoes** into
½-inch rounds (do not peel). Bake,
uncovered, for 30-35 minutes, until
tender-crisp. Cook meat as directed.
Using two forks, shred meat; top
sweet potatoes with shredded
brisket.

Serve as an appetizer.

Saucy Miami Ribs With Parsnips

MEAT I GLUTEN-FREE OPTION I FREEZES WELL I YIELDS 6 SERVINGS

INGREDIENTS

12 Miami beef ribs

4 medium parsnips
trimmed, peeled,
and halved lengthwise

kosher salt

black pepper

2 cloves garlic
minced (about 1 tsp)

⅓ cup soy sauce or tamari

¼ cup pure maple syrup

½ cup tomato sauce

⅓ cup water

⅓ cup chopped fresh parsley
plus more for garnish

METHOD

1 Preheat oven to 350°F. Coat
a large roasting pan with
nonstick cooking spray.

2 Arrange ribs and parsnips
in a single layer in prepared
pan. Sprinkle with salt and
pepper.

3 In a medium bowl, whisk
together garlic, soy sauce,
maple syrup, tomato sauce,
water, and parsley. Pour
mixture over ribs and
parsnips. Marinate for 1 hour
or overnight.

4   Bake, covered, for 1½-2 hours, or until meat is tender, basting occasionally.

5   Transfer to a large serving platter; garnish with additional parsley.

VARIATION

RIB APPETIZER

Cut ribs into individual pieces. Prepare recipe as directed. Serve individually plated over a bed of **rice, quinoa, rice noodles,** or **mashed potatoes.**

Brisket Ends

MEAT | GLUTEN-FREE OPTION | FREEZES WELL | YIELDS 8 SERVINGS

INGREDIENTS

1 beef brisket
(about 4 lb/2.3 kg)

2 Tbsp extra light olive oil

2 tsp kosher salt
or to taste

¼ tsp black pepper

2 tsp garlic powder

2 tsp onion powder

2 tsp smoked paprika

1 tsp dried thyme

1 cup BBQ sauce

3 Tbsp honey

2 Tbsp apple cider vinegar

METHOD

1   Preheat oven to 325°F. Coat a large roasting pan with nonstick cooking spray. Place roast into prepared baking pan.

2   Drizzle with oil, coating all sides; sprinkle with salt, pepper, garlic powder, onion powder, paprika, and thyme, massaging on all sides.

3   Bake, covered, for 3½-4 hours, until meat is
    fork-tender. Remove from oven; let cool for
    10-15 minutes.

4   Preheat oven to 375°F. Drain liquid from pan.

5   Cut meat into 2-inch cubes; return to pan.
    Pour on BBQ sauce, honey, and vinegar; mix
    to coat.

6   Bake, uncovered, for 30 minutes, until crispy
    on the edges.

VARIATION

BRISKET BOATS

Prepare recipe as directed. Serve
meat cubes in **romaine lettuce boats.**
Top with **sliced avocado, cherry
tomatoes,** or **veggies of your choice.**
Great as an appetizer or a carb-free
healthy dinner.

Smothered Short Ribs

MEAT I FREEZES WELL I YIELDS 6-8 SERVINGS

INGREDIENTS

12 beef short ribs/flanken
(about 6 lb/2.7 kg)
cut into individual ribs

kosher salt
to taste

black pepper
to taste

1 tsp sweet paprika

3 Tbsp tomato paste

3 Tbsp apple cider vinegar

3 Tbsp honey

1 Tbsp Worcestershire
sauce (fish-free)

1 tsp garlic powder

1 tsp onion powder

pinch chili powder

⅓ cup water or broth

METHOD

1   Coat a large roasting pan
    with nonstick cooking spray.
    Arrange individual short ribs
    in a single layer in prepared
    pan. Season ribs on all
    sides with salt, pepper, and
    paprika.

2   In a medium bowl, combine
    tomato paste, vinegar, honey,
    Worcestershire sauce, garlic
    powder, onion powder, chili
    powder, and water; mix well.

3   Pour sauce over and around ribs. Marinate for 20-30 minutes or overnight. in the fridge

4   Preheat oven to 350°F. Roast, covered, for 2 hours. Uncover; roast 15-20 minutes, until glazed and golden.

VARIATION

SHORT RIB CHUNKS WITH RICE

Prepare recipe as directed. Cook **2 cups rice** according to package directions. Add ⅓ cup rice to individual plates or bowls. Top with short rib chunks. Sprinkle with fresh **parsley** before serving.

Meatballs With Mushrooms

MEAT I GLUTEN-FREE I FREEZES WELL I YIELDS 6 SERVINGS

INGREDIENTS

SAUCE

1½ cups ketchup

2 cups soda water, Sprite,
or ginger ale

MEATBALLS

2 lb lean ground beef or
chicken

1 tsp kosher salt

¼ tsp black pepper

2 tsp onion powder

2 tsp garlic powder

2 tsp sweet paprika

¼ tsp dried thyme

4 cups button mushrooms
trimmed (do not slice)

METHOD

1   Sauce: In a large saucepan
over medium heat, combine
ketchup and soda water; stir
well. Bring to a boil.

2   Meanwhile, prepare the
meatballs. In a large bowl,
combine ground beef with
salt, pepper, onion powder,
garlic powder, paprika,
and thyme. Mix lightly to
combine. Do not overmix or
meatballs will be tough.

3   Form meat mixture into 2-inch balls, wetting your hands for easier shaping. Add meatballs and mushrooms to simmering sauce. Then shake pot back and forth gently so meatballs are covered with sauce.

4   Let simmer, partially covered, for 50-60 minutes, until sauce has thickened.

VARIATION

MEATBALL MUSHROOM SLOPPY JOES

Combine ground beef with chopped mushrooms. Heat 2 tablespoons **oil** in skillet; add meat mixture and spices. Sauté 5-7 minutes, until browned. Stir in ketchup and soda water. Bring to a boil; reduce heat and simmer for 50-60 minutes. Serve over **rice, spaghetti squash**, **hotdog buns**, etc. (Sauce inspired by Norene Gilletz.)

Overnight Shabbos Corned Beef

MEAT I GLUTEN-FREE I YIELDS 6 SERVINGS

INGREDIENTS

1 pickled corned beef
(about 2 lb)

1 Tbsp ground coriander

1½ tsp dry mustard

1 Tbsp sweet paprika

2 tsp garlic powder

2 tsp onion powder

2 Tbsp brown sugar

2 Tbsp extra light olive oil

METHOD

1   Bring a large pot of water
to a boil. Rinse meat well to
remove excess spices. Add
meat to pot; simmer, partially
covered, for 2 hours, or until
fork tender. Drain; let cool
slightly.

2   Preheat oven to 200°F.

3   Place corned beef into a resealable plastic cooking bag. Season with coriander, mustard, paprika, garlic powder, onion powder, brown sugar, and oil; rub to coat on all sides. Press out air from bag; seal tightly.

4   Place meat into a large ovenproof pot, being careful not to puncture the bag. Add water until meat is almost covered. Cover pot; place into oven. Slow cook for 8-10 hours or overnight.

5   Carefully remove from oven. Remove meat from bag. Discard liquid. Cool. Slice on an angle against the grain.

VARIATION

CLUB SANDWICHES

Prepare recipe as directed. Using **sliced challah bread,** assemble sandwiches using the overnight meat. Toppings can include **lettuce, tomatoes, pickles, red onion, deli mustard, Dijon mustard,** etc. Serve on a large platter or on individual plates as an appetizer.

Taco Bowl Night

MEAT I GLUTEN-FREE I YIELDS 4-6 SERVINGS

INGREDIENTS

1-2 Tbsp grapeseed oil

1 lb lean ground beef
or chicken

1 tsp chili powder

1 tsp kosher salt
or to taste

1 tsp ground cumin

½ tsp dried oregano

1 tsp garlic powder

1 tsp onion powder

¾ cup tomato sauce or
marinara sauce

1 cup basmati rice

TOPPING SUGGESTIONS

1 cup shelled edamame
beans

2 firm tomatoes, diced

1 firm Hass avocado
peeled, pitted, and diced

1 cup crushed tortilla chips

hot sauce or spicy mayo

METHOD

1   In large nonstick wok or
skillet, heat oil over medium
high heat; add meat. Sauté
for 5 minutes, until browned,
stirring to break up chunks.

2   Add chili powder, salt, cumin,
oregano, garlic powder,
onion powder, and tomato
sauce. Cook for 12-15
minutes, stirring often, until
beef is fully cooked.

3   Meanwhile, cook rice according to package
    directions.

4   Assembly: Spoon ½-cup rice into individual
    bowls. Divide the ground beef and topping of
    your choice between bowls. Drizzle with hot
    sauce.

VARIATION

TACO DINNER

Prepare recipe as directed through
Step 3. Fill **hard-shelled tacos** with
rice, meat, and toppings.

DAIRY

Pull-Apart Eggplant Parmesan

DAIRY I PASSOVER I GLUTEN-FREE I YIELDS 4-6 SERVINGS

INGREDIENTS

1½ cups marinara sauce

1 large eggplant

10-15 slices yellow or white cheese

1 cup shredded mozzarella cheese

2 cloves garlic
minced (about 1 tsp)

⅓ cup chopped flat leaf parsley
plus more for garnish

METHOD

1   Preheat oven to 400°F. Coat a 9 x 13-inch glass or ceramic baking dish with nonstick cooking spray. Spoon the marinara sauce into the dish.

2   Using a serrated knife, carefully cut ½-inch widthwise slits into eggplant, cutting almost to the bottom, but not cutting fully through. Place eggplant into prepared dish.

3   Place a cheese slice into each eggplant slit.
     Bake, covered, for 40-45 minutes, until
     eggplant has softened.

4   Uncover; sprinkle with shredded cheese,
     garlic, and parsley. Bake 10-15 minutes, until
     cheese is golden and bubbling. Garnish with
     additional parsley.

5   Plate each serving with a few slices of
     eggplant along with pan sauce.

VARIATION

BABY EGGPLANT PARMESAN

Use 5-6 **baby eggplants** for
individual servings. Prepare recipe as
directed, dividing cheese, garlic, and
parsley between eggplants. Bake,
uncovered, for 30-35 minutes.

Great for an easy dinner or for
Shavuot.

Low-Cal Cauliflower Mushroom Risotto

DAIRY I GLUTEN-FREE I YIELDS 4 SERVINGS

INGREDIENTS

1-2 Tbsp extra light olive oil

1 medium red onion
diced

2 cloves garlic
minced (about 1 tsp)

2 cups sliced button
mushrooms

1 pkg (14 oz/397 g) riced
cauliflower (about 4 cups)

1½ tsp kosher salt
or to taste

black pepper

⅓ cup grated Parmesan
cheese

⅓ cup shredded mozzarella
cheese

3 Tbsp chopped fresh dill

METHOD

1 In a large frying pan, heat
   oil over medium-high heat.
   Add onion, garlic, and
   mushrooms; stir-fry for 5-7
   minutes, until tender-crisp.
   Transfer to a serving bowl.

2   In the same frying pan, stir together cauliflower "rice," salt, pepper, Parmesan cheese, mozzarella, and dill. Cook for 2-4 minutes, until cheeses are melted. Add to serving bowl; adjust seasonings to taste. Toss to combine. Serve immediately.

VARIATION

RISOTTO BALLS

Preheat oven to 400°F. Line a rimmed baking sheet with parchment paper. Prepare recipe as directed, but finely dice mushrooms. Let cool. Form mixture into 1-inch balls; roll balls in 1 cup **panko crumbs**, coating all sides. Place balls on prepared baking sheet. Brush with 2-3 Tbsp **oil.** Bake, uncovered, for 5-8 minutes, until golden. Alternatively, the cauliflower "balls" can be fried in oil for 2-3 minutes per side, until golden.

Summery Feta Salad

DAIRY I GLUTEN-FREE I YIELDS 8 SERVINGS

INGREDIENTS

4-6 cups chopped frisée lettuce

1 cup shredded red cabbage

1 cup fresh blueberries

1 cup diced nectarines or peaches

1 cup sliced radishes

1 avocado

1 cup crumbled feta cheese

⅓ cup chopped fresh mint

½ cup shelled pistachios
optional

DRESSING

⅓ cup light olive oil

zest of 2 lemons

juice of 2 lemons

1 tsp kosher salt

black pepper

METHOD

1 In a medium bowl, combine lettuce with cabbage, blueberries, nectarines, and radishes. Cover and refrigerate.

2 Dressing: Combine dressing ingredients in a glass jar; seal tightly and shake well. Refrigerate.

3   Shortly before serving, peel, pit, and dice avocado. Add to salad along with feta, mint, and dressing. Stir gently to combine. Sprinkle with pistachios, if using. Serve immediately.

VARIATION

ROMAINE FETA SALAD

Prepare recipe as directed, using 4-6 cups chopped **romaine lettuce** in place of the frisée. Alternatively, use **spinach**. This is a great brunch or Shavuot recipe.

Zoodle Cheese Nests

DAIRY I PASSOVER I GLUTEN-FREE I YIELDS 20-25 NESTS

INGREDIENTS

2-3 containers (12 oz/340 g) spiralized zucchini, squash, beets, or carrots

1 cup marinara sauce

2-3 cups shredded Cheddar cheese

METHOD

1 Preheat oven to 350°F. Line a rimmed baking sheet with parchment paper.

2   Gather a handful of zoodles and rotate your hand while placing them onto prepared pan, forming a circular nest. Top with 2-3 Tbsp marinara sauce; sprinkle with cheese. Repeat with remaining zoodles, sauce, and cheese.

3   Bake, uncovered, for 15-18 minutes, until bubbling.

VARIATION

ZOODLE LASAGNA

Preheat oven to 350°F. Coat the bottom of a 9 x 13-inch glass or ceramic baking dish with nonstick cooking spray. Spoon ½ cup marinara sauce into dish; sprinkle with half the cheese. Top with zoodles. Add a second layer of marinara sauce; top with cheese. Bake, uncovered, for 25-35 minutes, until piping hot.

Crustless Baby Red Potato Quiche

DAIRY I PASSOVER I GLUTEN- FREE I YIELDS 8 SERVINGS

INGREDIENTS

15-20 small red potatoes
*thinly sliced into rounds
(do not peel)*

½ cup milk

4 eggs

½ cup crumbled feta cheese

1 cup shredded Cheddar or
mozzarella cheese

½ tsp chopped fresh
rosemary or thyme
plus more for garnish

1½ tsp kosher salt

black pepper

METHOD

1   Preheat oven to 350°F. Coat
the bottom and sides of a
10-inch glass or ceramic
baking dish with nonstick
cooking spray.

2   In a large bowl, combine potatoes with milk,
    eggs, feta, Cheddar cheese, rosemary, salt,
    and pepper; mix well. Pour into prepared
    baking dish. Garnish top with additional herbs.

3   Bake, uncovered, for 40-45 minutes, until
    potatoes are tender.

VARIATION

MINI POTATO TARTS

Prepare recipe as directed. Put ¼-⅓-
cup mixture into individual ramekins
or lined muffin tins. Bake, uncovered,
for 25-30 minutes, or until golden
and set.

Cheesy Seed Crisps

DAIRY I GLUTEN-FREE I FREEZES WELL I YIELDS 15-18 CRISPS

INGREDIENTS

½ cup shelled
pumpkin seeds
(salted or unsalted)

½ cup shelled
sunflower seeds
(salted or unsalted)

¼ cup uncooked quinoa
(any color)

2 Tbsp sesame seeds
(white or black)

2 Tbsp flax seeds, hemp
hearts, or chia seeds

1 Tbsp extra light olive oil

1 tsp kosher salt

2 cups shredded mozzarella
or Cheddar cheese

METHOD

1   Preheat oven to 400°F. Line
    2 rimmed baking sheets or
    pizza pans with parchment
    paper.

2   In a medium bowl, combine all ingredients. Spoon about ¼-cup mixture onto prepared baking sheet. Spread into a 2-3-inch circle. Repeat with remaining cheese mixture.

3   Bake, uncovered, for 10-15 minutes, until cheese is bubbling and golden, making sure crisps do not burn. Cool completely.

4   Plate cheese crisps on a cheese board to serve.

VARIATION

CAESAR CRISP SALAD

Break cheesy Seed Crisps onto a **Caesar salad** or top salad with whole crisps as a garnish

Keto Cheese Crust Pizza

DAIRY I PASSOVER I GLUTEN-FREE I YIELDS 4 SERVINGS

INGREDIENTS

1½ cups shredded
mozzarella cheese

2 Tbsp Parmesan cheese

½ tsp dried basil

pinch kosher salt

2 eggs

1 cup pizza sauce

1-2 cups veggies
(e.g., mushrooms, onions, olives)

METHOD

1 Preheat oven to 350°F. Line
a pizza pan or baking sheet
with parchment paper.

2 In a medium bowl, combine
cheeses with basil, salt, and
eggs; mix well.

3 Spread mixture evenly onto
prepared baking sheet,
forming a large circle. Press
down on the mixture with a
second piece of parchment
paper to thin it to about
½ inch.

4   Bake, uncovered, for about 20 minutes or until edges are deep golden.

5   Raise oven temperature to 400°F. Remove pan from oven; top crust with pizza sauce and your favorite vegetable toppings.

6   Return to oven; bake about 10 minutes or until veggies have softened.

VARIATION

INDIVIDUAL PIZZAS

Line a large baking sheet or pizza pan with parchment paper. After completing Steps 1 and 2, use about ⅓-cup cheese mixture to create individual pizza crusts. Bake crusts for 12-15 minutes until golden. Turn oven temperature to 400°F. Top with veggies; bake 10 minutes.

Granola Crusted "Breakfast" Tart

DAIRY I GLUTEN-FREE OPTION I YIELDS 6 SERVINGS

INGREDIENTS

1½ cups large flake oats
(gluten free or regular)

⅓ cup slivered almonds

¼ cup shredded
sweetened coconut

¼ cup honey

3 Tbsp oil or coconut oil

1 tsp pure vanilla extract

1 egg white

FILLING

2 cups Greek yogurt

2 cups assorted berries

honey
for drizzling

METHOD

1   Preheat oven to 350°F. Line a 9-inch round tart pan with removable bottom with parchment paper; coat the sides with nonstick cooking spray.

2   In a large bowl, combine oats with almonds, coconut, honey, oil, vanilla, and egg white; mix well. Spoon mixture into prepared pan, spreading it up the sides to create a crust.

3   Bake, uncovered, for 20-25 minutes, until
    golden. Let cool completely.

4   Spread with Greek yogurt; top with assorted
    berries. Drizzle with honey. Serve immediately.

VARIATION

YOGURT PARFAIT

Line a baking sheet with parchment
paper. Prepare granola crust as
directed. Spoon onto prepared baking
sheet. Bake, uncovered, for 20-25
minutes. Cool. Break into irregular
pieces. Use as a topping for yogurt.
Add berries or **fresh fruit.**

Baked Broccoli Tots

DAIRY I GLUTEN-FREE OPTION I FREEZES WELL I YIELDS ABOUT 2 DOZEN

INGREDIENTS

4 cups broccoli florets
(fresh or frozen)

1 large onion, chopped

2 cloves garlic
minced (about 1 tsp)

3 eggs

1 cup unseasoned
panko crumbs
(gluten-free or regular)

⅔ cup shredded
mozzarella cheese

¼ cup chopped
fresh parsley

1½ tsp kosher salt

¼ tsp black pepper

METHOD

1 Preheat oven to 400°F.
Line a baking sheet with
parchment paper.

2 Using a food processer fitted
with the "S" blade, process
broccoli, onion, and garlic
until somewhat smooth.

3 In a mixing bowl, combine
broccoli mixture with eggs,
panko, cheese, parsley, salt,
and pepper; mix well.

4   Gently press 1 tablespoon of mixture between your hands to form a tater tot shape. Place onto prepared baking sheet. Repeat with remaining mixture.

5   Bake, uncovered, for 15 minutes or until slightly golden.

VARIATION

BROCCOLI TART

Prepare recipe as directed through Step 3. Coat a 9- or 10-inch round ceramic or glass baking dish with nonstick cooking spray. Spoon mixture into prepared dish; spread evenly. Bake, uncovered, for 15-20 minutes, until golden. Yields 8 servings.

5-Ingredient Cauliflower Cheese Bites

DAIRY I PASSOVER I GLUTEN-FREE I FREEZES WELL I YIELDS 2 DOZEN

INGREDIENTS

2 cups cauliflower "rice"
fresh or frozen

1½ cups shredded
mozzarella or
Cheddar cheese

1 tsp black pepper

2 eggs

1 tsp salt

METHOD

1   Preheat oven to 400°F. Coat
mini muffin compartments
with nonstick cooking spray.

2   In a medium bowl, combine
cauliflower, cheese, pepper,
eggs, and salt; mix well.
Place 1-2 tablespoons
mixture into each muffin
compartment.

3   Bake, uncovered, for 15-20
minutes, until golden.

VARIATION

CAULIFLOWER QUICHE

Prepare recipe as directed through Step 2. Coat a glass or ceramic 9- or 10-inch baking dish with nonstick cooking spray. Spread cauliflower mixture evenly into prepared baking dish. Bake, uncovered, for 30-35 minutes, until browned.

Yields 6 servings.

Avocado Pesto Spaghetti

DAIRY I GLUTEN-FREE OPTION I YIELDS 6-8 SERVINGS

INGREDIENTS

1 pkg (16 oz/454 g) **spaghetti** (gluten-free or regular)

1 pkg (12 oz/340 g) **frozen shelled edamame beans**

1 ripe Hass avocado

⅓ cup grated Parmesan cheese

PESTO

1 Hass avocado

1 cup fresh basil

1 cup fresh flat leaf parsley

⅓ cup fresh walnuts
optional

1 clove garlic

2 Tbsp lemon juice
(preferably fresh)

1 tsp kosher salt

¼ tsp black pepper

2-3 Tbsp water

¼ cup extra light olive oil

METHOD

1 Cook pasta al dente in salted water according to package directions. Drain well.

2 Transfer pasta to a serving bowl; let cool.

3   Bring a medium saucepan of salted water
    to a boil. Add edamame beans; boil for 3-5
    minutes, until tender-crisp. Drain well.

4   Pesto: In a food processor, process avocado,
    basil, parsley, walnuts (if using), garlic, lemon
    juice, salt, and pepper until smooth. With
    machine running, gradually add water and
    olive oil until mixture is smooth.

5   Peel, pit, and dice avocado. Add to pasta
    along with pesto, edamame beans, and
    Parmesan cheese. Mix well. Adjust seasonings
    to taste.

VARIATION

ELBOW NOODLE PESTO

Prepare recipe as directed, using
elbow noodles instead of spaghetti.
Serve in individual ramekins.

Great for kids.

Lazy Hash and Egg Dinner

DAIRY I PASSOVER I GLUTEN-FREE I YIELDS 4 SERVINGS

INGREDIENTS

2 Tbsp extra light olive oil

1 cup finely diced red onion

2 cloves garlic
minced (about 1 tsp)

1 cup finely diced
sweet potato (do not peel)

1 cup finely diced parsnip

1 cup finely diced
cooked beets

1½ tsp kosher salt

black pepper

1 tsp smoked paprika

4 eggs

1 cup feta cheese

1 cup roughly chopped
spinach

METHOD

1   In a large frying pan, heat
oil over medium-high heat.
Add onion and garlic; sauté
for 5-7 minutes, until onions
have softened.

2   Add sweet potato, parsnip,
beets, salt, pepper, and
paprika; cook for 12-15
minutes until vegetables are
tender-crisp.

3   Make 4 indentations in the vegetable mixture, leaving room between each space. Working with 1 egg at a time, crack egg into a small bowl or cup. Slip egg into an indentation; season with salt and pepper. Repeat with remaining eggs.

4   Scatter on feta cheese and spinach. Lightly cover the frying pan with foil. Cook for 5-7 minutes, or until eggs are cooked but yolks still runny. Serve immediately.

VARIATION

FETA QUINOA HASH

Cook 1 cup white or red **quinoa**, as directed on package. Prepare vegetables as in Steps 1-2. Omit Steps 3-4. Toss quinoa with vegetables, feta, and spinach before serving. Great for a dairy brunch.

GRAIN SIDES

Crispy Garlic Couscous

PAREVE I GLUTEN-FREE OPTION I YIELDS 6 SERVINGS

INGREDIENTS

1½ cups couscous

TOPPING

2 Tbsp extra light olive oil

1 large red onion
diced

6 cloves garlic
minced (about 2 Tbsp)

2 tsp kosher salt

black pepper

1½ cups panko crumbs
(gluten-free or regular)

3 Tbsp fresh
chopped parsley
plus more for garnish

METHOD

1   Cook 1½ cups couscous
    according to package
    directions. Fluff with a
    fork. Place into individual
    ramekins or a large serving
    bowl.

2   Heat oil in a large skillet. Add
    onion and garlic; sauté for
    5-7 minutes, until softened.

3   Add salt, pepper, panko
    crumbs, and parsley; toast
    for 3-4 minutes. Spoon
    topping over couscous.

VARIATION

PANKO GARLIC CHERRY TOMATOES

Combine panko topping ingredients in large bowl; mix well. Coat a 10-inch round baking dish with nonstick cooking spray. Add 3-4 cups **cherry tomatoes**. Sprinkle with salt and pepper. Top with panko topping. Bake at 375°F, uncovered, for 30-40 minutes, until topping is golden.

Jasmine Coconut and Cranberry Rice

PAREVE I GLUTEN-FREE I YIELDS 6 SERVINGS

INGREDIENTS

1½ cups jasmine rice
rinsed well

2 Tbsp extra light olive oil or
coconut oil

½ cup finely chopped mint

1½ cups sweetened toasted
coconut flakes

¾ cup slivered or sliced
almonds
toasted

½ cup dried cranberries

1 tsp kosher salt

black pepper

METHOD

1   Cook rice according to
package directions. Fluff
with a fork. Let cool slightly.

2   Transfer rice to a large bowl. Add oil, mint,
    coconut, almonds, cranberries, salt, and
    pepper; mix well.

VARIATION

COCONUT BOWLS

Prepare recipe as directed. Serve in
halved coconuts. You can ask at your
local fruit store to cut them in half.

Candied Brown Rice Salad

PAREVE | GLUTEN-FREE | YIELDS 4-6 SERVINGS

INGREDIENTS

CRUNCH

2 Tbsp extra light olive oil

⅓ cup pumpkin seeds

⅓ cup sunflower seeds

½ cup slivered almonds

2 Tbsp hemp hearts

1 Tbsp honey

SALAD

1 cup brown rice

1 cup shelled edamame beans

2 cups arugula

DRESSING

2 Tbsp extra light olive oil

2 Tbsp red wine vinegar

kosher salt

black pepper

METHOD

1   Crunch: Preheat oven to 350°F. Line a rimmed baking sheet with parchment paper.

2   In a small bowl, combine oil, pumpkin seeds, sunflower seeds, almonds, hemp hearts, and honey; mix well. Spread out evenly on prepared baking sheet.

3   Bake, uncovered, for 12-15 minutes, until golden. Let cool.

4   Salad: Cook rice according to package directions. Fluff with a fork; let cool.

5   Meanwhile, cook shelled edamame beans in boiling water for 3-5 minutes until tender-crisp. Drain well.

6   Transfer rice to a serving bowl. Add arugula and edamame beans.

7   Dressing: Combine dressing ingredients in a glass jar; seal tightly and shake well.

8   Stir dressing into rice mixture.

9   Break seeded crunch into irregular-sized pieces; scatter over rice salad.

VARIATION

CRUNCH TOPPING

Omit rice. Use this topping over salads, yogurt, or ice cream; or enjoy it as a snack.

Mediterranean Quinoa Salad

PAREVE I GLUTEN-FREE I YIELDS 6-8 SERVINGS

INGREDIENTS

1 small eggplant
trimmed and diced (do not peel)

1 large sweet potato
trimmed and diced (do not peel)

2 Tbsp extra light olive oil

kosher salt

black pepper

3 cups lightly salted water

1½ cups quinoa

1 can (19 oz/540 ml) chickpeas
drained, rinsed, and patted dry

¾ cup sliced green or black olives

5 pickles
trimmed and sliced

½ cup halved cherry tomatoes

½ cup slivered or sliced almonds
toasted

1 firm Hass avocado

½ cup tahini or hummus

METHOD

1   Preheat oven to 400°F. Line a large rimmed baking sheet with parchment paper.

2   Spread diced eggplant and sweet potato on prepared baking sheet in a single layer. Drizzle with oil; sprinkle with salt and pepper.

3   Roast, uncovered, for 35-40 minutes, or until tender.

4   Meanwhile, bring water to a boil in a medium saucepan over high heat. Add quinoa; reduce heat. Simmer, covered, for 15 minutes, or until tender. Let stand for 10 minutes. Fluff quinoa with a fork. Transfer to a large serving bowl.

5   Add eggplant, sweet potatoes, chickpeas, olives, pickles, tomatoes, and almonds to bowl; mix well.

6   Shortly before serving, peel, pit, and dice the avocado. Add to quinoa mixture; mix well. Drizzle with tahini.

VARIATION

QUINOA BOWL

Prepare recipe as directed. Arrange all ingredients in individual serving bowls. Drizzle with tahini before serving.

Spicy Roasted Cauliflower and Chickpea Salad

PAREVE I GLUTEN-FREE I YIELDS 6 SERVINGS

INGREDIENTS

1 head cauliflower
cut into large florets

1 can (19 oz/540 ml) chickpeas
rinsed and drained

2 Tbsp extra light olive oil

2 tsp chili powder

2 tsp sweet paprika

1 tsp kosher salt

¼ tsp ground cumin

2 avocados

½ cup chopped fresh
parsley or cilantro

juice of 1 lemon

METHOD

1   Preheat oven to 400°F. Line
a rimmed baking sheet with
parchment paper.

2   In a medium bowl, combine
cauliflower, chickpeas, oil,
chili powder, paprika, salt,
and cumin; mix well.

3   Arrange in a single layer on prepared baking sheet. Roast, uncovered, for 30-35 minutes, until golden.

4   Transfer to serving dish. Shortly before serving, peel, pit, and dice avocados; add to cauliflower mixture along with parsley and juice of a lemon. Serve hot or at room temperature.

VARIATION

LENTIL CAULIFLOWER SALAD

Prepare recipe as directed, using 1 can (19 oz/540 ml) **brown lentils** in place of chickpeas.

Asian Rice Salad With Wasabi Peas

PAREVE I GLUTEN-FREE OPTION I YIELDS 6-8 SERVINGS

INGREDIENTS

½ pkg (10 oz/300 g)
thin rice noodles

1 pkg (16 oz/500 g)
sliced red cabbage

3 scallions
thinly sliced

1 cup peanuts
(salted or unsalted)

1 cup green or
white wasabi peas
(regular or gluten-free)

DRESSING

⅓ cup extra light olive oil

¼ cup soy sauce or tamari

3 Tbsp rice vinegar

2 Tbsp honey

1 tsp kosher salt
or to taste

black pepper

METHOD

1   Cook rice noodles according
to package directions;
this will take only about 2
minutes to cook. Drain well.
Place into a large serving
bowl; cut into 2-inch strands.

2   Add red cabbage, scallions, and peanuts.
    Cover; refrigerate.

3   Dressing: Combine dressing ingredients in a
    glass jar; seal tightly and shake well.

4   Shortly before serving, toss salad with
    dressing and wasabi peas.

VARIATION

CHINESE BOX RICE SALAD

Prepare recipe as directed. Place
about ½-cup rice salad into Chinese
boxes for a cute appetizer idea or for
a party. Serve with chopsticks.

Roasted Onion Quinoa Salad

PAREVE I GLUTEN-FREE I YIELDS 8 SERVING

INGREDIENTS

2 medium red onions
trimmed, halved, and sliced

2 white onions
trimmed, halved, and sliced

2 Tbsp extra light olive oil

kosher salt

black pepper

2 cups salted water

1 cup white quinoa

½ cup pumpkin seeds

2 avocados

DRESSING

⅓ cup extra light olive oil

juice and zest of 2 lemons

1½ tsp kosher salt

black pepper

¼ cup chopped fresh mint

METHOD

1 Preheat oven to 400°F. Line a large rimmed baking sheet with parchment paper.

2 Spread onions on prepared baking sheet. Drizzle with oil; sprinkle with salt and pepper.

3 Roast, uncovered, for 35-40 minutes, or until browned.

4   Meanwhile, bring water to a boil in a medium saucepan over high heat. Add quinoa; reduce heat. Simmer, covered, for 15 minutes, or until tender. Remove from heat; let stand for 10 minutes; covered. Fluff quinoa with a fork. Transfer to a large serving bowl.

5   Add pumpkin seeds and roasted onions to quinoa. Mix to combine.

6   Combine dressing ingredients in a glass jar; seal tightly and shake well.

7   Shortly before serving, peel, pit, and dice the avocados. Add to salad with the dressing.

VARIATION

COLORFUL QUINOA SALAD

Prepare recipe as directed using different colors of quinoa (e.g., black, red, or a combo of both). You can also add 1 can (19 oz/540 ml) **lentils** or **chickpeas**.

Fresh Orzo Salad

PAREVE I YIELDS 8 SERVINGS

INGREDIENTS

1 pkg (12 oz/340 g) **orzo**
(rice-shaped pasta)

1 can (19 oz/ 540 ml) **chickpeas**
rinsed, drained, and patted dry

½ cup finely diced red onion

3 baby cucumbers
trimmed and diced

⅓ cup chopped fresh mint

⅓ cup chopped fresh basil

⅓ cup extra light olive oil

zest and juice of 2 limes

1 tsp kosher salt

black pepper

**½ cup chopped candied
pecans or cashews**

METHOD

1   Cook orzo in salted water
    according to package
    directions. Drain well.
    Transfer to a large serving
    bowl.

2   Add chickpeas, onion,
    cucumbers, mint, and basil.

3   Drizzle in oil, lime zest, lime
    juice, salt, and pepper; toss
    to combine. Top with candied
    nuts. Serve hot, cold or at
    room temperature.

VARIATION

ORZO PEPPER CUPS

Prepare salad as directed. Halve
4 **bell peppers** (any color); remove
seeds. Shortly before serving, spoon
in ¼-⅓-cup orzo salad. Serve as a
plated appetizer.

Crouton Farro Salad

PAREVE I YIELDS 6 SERVINGS

INGREDIENTS

1 cup pearled farro

1 cup shredded red cabbage

1 cup diced mango

1 bunch chives, chopped

⅓ cup small soup croutons

DRESSING

⅓ cup extra light olive oil

2 Tbsp balsamic vinegar

1 Tbsp Dijon mustard

1 tsp honey

kosher salt

black pepper

METHOD

1 Cook farro according to package directions. Drain well; let cool. Transfer to a serving bowl.

2 Add cabbage, mango, and chives to farro; cover and refrigerate.

3   Combine dressing ingredients in a glass jar;
    seal tightly and shake well.

4   Shortly before serving, add dressing to salad;
    toss gently to combine. Top with croutons.

VARIATION

BARLEY POKE BOWL

Prepare recipe as directed, using
1 cup **barley** in place of farro. Arrange
barley and vegetables in a serving
bowl. Sprinkle with chives; drizzle
with dressing.

VEGETABLE
SIDES

Garlic Shishito Peppers

PAREVE I PASSOVER I GLUTEN-FREE I YIELDS 8 SERVINGS

INGREDIENTS

2 pkg (8 oz/ 227 g each) whole shishito peppers

2 Tbsp extra light olive oil

kosher salt

black pepper

1 tsp garlic powder

METHOD

1 Preheat a grill or grill pan to high.

2 In a medium bowl, combine peppers with oil, salt, pepper, and garlic powder; mix well.

3　Grill on a barbeque grill or a grill pan for 2-3 minutes per side, until slightly charred.

4　Transfer to a bowl; serve as a side dish.

VARIATION

SHISHITO BOARD

Prepare recipe as directed. Place grilled peppers onto a wooden cutting board. Add an assortment of **pickles, asparagus, olives,** and **pickled peppers** or **bell peppers.**

Maple-Glazed Japanese Sweet Potatoes

PAREVE I GLUTEN-FREE I YIELDS 4-6 SERVINGS

INGREDIENTS

3 large Japanese
sweet potatoes
*trimmed and cut into wedges
(do not peel)*

1 tsp kosher salt

1 tsp ground cinnamon

2-3 Tbsp extra light olive oil

2 Tbsp pure maple syrup

METHOD

1   Preheat oven to 400°F. Line
a rimmed baking sheet with
parchment paper.

2   Spread potato wedges in
a single layer on prepared
baking sheet.

3   Sprinkle with salt and cinnamon. Drizzle with oil and maple syrup, tossing to coat on all sides.

4   Bake, uncovered, for 35-45 minutes, until golden and crispy. Wedges should be tender when pierced with a fork. Transfer to a serving platter; serve hot or at room temperature.

VARIATION

SALAD BOWLS

Prepare recipe as directed. Place **1 cup lettuce greens** and **½ cup veggies** (e.g., cucumbers, peppers, tomatoes) into individual salad bowls or plates. Cut sweet potatoes into 1-inch pieces; place onto salad. Use the dressing from Panko-Topped Kale Salad on page 70.

Enjoy for lunch the next day or serve as an appetizer.

Lemon-Mint Mini Peppers

PAREVE I GLUTEN-FREE I YIELDS 4-6 PEOPLE

INGREDIENTS

2 (14-16 oz each) pkg mini
sweet peppers (assorted
colors)
washed (do not trim)

1-2 Tbsp extra light olive oil

juice of ½ lemon
(about 2 Tbsp)

2 Tbsp honey

2 cloves garlic
minced (about 1 tsp)

⅓ cup chopped fresh mint
or basil

½ tsp kosher salt

¼ tsp black pepper

METHOD

1   Preheat oven to 400°F. Line
    a rimmed baking sheet with
    parchment paper.

2   In a large bowl, combine
    peppers with oil, lemon juice,
    honey, garlic, mint, salt, and
    pepper. Toss well to coat.

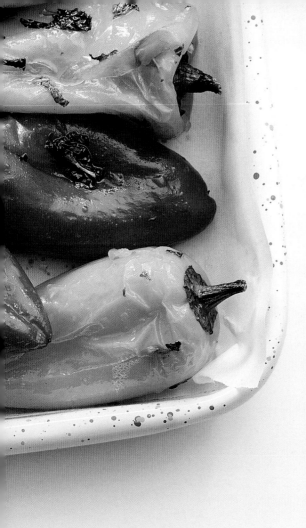

3   Transfer peppers and marinade to prepared baking sheet; spread into a single layer.

4   Roast, uncovered, for 20-25 minutes, until lightly charred.

VARIATION

ROASTED PEPPER WRAPS

Prepare recipe as directed. Remove stem from peppers and place into small or large **wraps**. Add **greens, diced avocado,** and **cucumbers,** or **veggies** of your choice.

Great to serve at a brunch.

"Everything Bagel" Asparagus

PAREVE I GLUTEN-FREE I YIELDS 6-8 SERVINGS

INGREDIENTS

2 bunches asparagus
(about 2 lb/1 kg each)

2 Tbsp sesame seeds
(black, white, or both)

1 Tbsp poppy seeds

1½ Tbsp dried minced garlic

1½ Tbsp dried
minced onion

1 tsp flaked sea salt

2 Tbsp extra light olive oil

METHOD

1   Preheat oven to 400°F. Line
a rimmed baking sheet with
parchment paper. Spread
asparagus in a single layer
on prepared baking sheet

2   In a small bowl, combine
sesame seeds, poppy seeds,
minced garlic, minced onion,
and salt; mix well.

3   Drizzle asparagus with oil; sprinkle with sesame seed mixture, coating all sides.

4   Roast, uncovered, for 10-12 minutes, or until tender-crisp.

VARIATION

ASPARAGUS AND RICE

Prepare recipe as directed. Cook **1½ cups rice** according to package directions; transfer to a large serving bowl. Cut cooked asparagus into 1-inch pieces; add to rice, mixing well. Serve hot or at room temperature.

Spiced Eggplant Wedges

PAREVE I GLUTEN-FREE I YIELDS 4-6 SERVINGS

INGREDIENTS

1 large eggplant
ends trimmed (do not peel)

2 Tbsp extra light olive oil

1 Tbsp soy sauce or tamari

1 Tbsp pure maple syrup

1 tsp sweet paprika

1 tsp garlic powder

1 tsp kosher salt

¼ tsp black pepper

METHOD

1   Preheat oven to 400°F. Line a rimmed baking sheet with parchment paper.

2   Cut eggplant in half widthwise, then into wedges, forming 8 wedges in total. Spread out in a single layer on prepared baking sheet.

3   In a small bowl, combine oil, soy sauce, maple
    syrup, paprika, garlic powder, salt, and pepper;
    mix well.

4   Using a pastry brush, brush eggplant wedges
    evenly on both sides with mixture. Repeat
    until all remaining mixture has been used.

5   Bake, uncovered, for 25-30 minutes, or until
    edges are crispy. Transfer to a serving platter.

VARIATION

HUMMUS EGGPLANT TOPPER

Dice eggplant into bite-size pieces.
Prepare recipe as directed. Place 1½
cups **hummus** into a serving bowl;
top with diced eggplant. Sprinkle with
2 Tbsp fresh leaf **parsley**.

Pretty Roasted Onion Flowers

PAREVE I PASSOVER I GLUTEN-FREE I YIELDS 6 SERVINGS

INGREDIENTS

6 small red onions
trimmed and peeled

6 Tbsp extra light olive oil
divided

kosher salt
to taste

black pepper
to taste

2 Tbsp chopped fresh
thyme or rosemary
plus more for garnish

METHOD

1 Preheat oven to 350°F. Line
   a rimmed baking sheet with
   parchment paper.

2 Make 4 vertical cuts into
   each onion, creating 8
   wedges — be careful not
   to cut into the root end or
   the onions won't hold their
   flower shape!

3 Place onions on prepared
   baking sheet, root-side
   down.

VARIATION

ONION GARNISH

Prepare recipe as directed. These pretty onions are great as a garnish to any dish. Place them alongside your meat, chicken, or fish to enhance the presentation.

4 Drizzle 3 tablespoons oil between onion wedges; sprinkle generously with salt and pepper.

5 Roast, uncovered, for about 30 minutes, until onions "bloom" as the wedges open outward.

6 Remove from oven; drizzle with remaining oil. Sprinkle with additional salt and pepper; top with herbs.

7 Return to oven; roast for 20-25 minutes, until onions are tender on the inside and tips are crispy. Remove from oven and garnish with more herbs before serving.

Chip-Topped Green Beans

PAREVE I GLUTEN-FREE I YIELDS 6-8 SERVINGS

INGREDIENTS

12 mini red potatoes
*scrubbed and thinly sliced
(do not peel)*

4 Tbsp extra light olive oil
divided

kosher salt
to taste

black pepper
to taste

2 lb/1 kg thin green beans
(haricots verts) ends trimmed

3 Tbsp soy sauce or tamari

pinch kosher salt

black pepper
to taste

METHOD

1   Preheat oven to 425°F. Line a rimmed baking sheet with parchment paper.

2   Scatter potato slices in a single layer on prepared baking sheet. Drizzle with 2 tablespoons oil; sprinkle with salt and pepper. Toss gently to combine.

3   Roast, uncovered, for 20-25 minutes, until golden and crunchy.

4   Meanwhile, in a nonstick wok, heat remaining 2 tablespoons oil over medium-high heat. Add green beans; stir-fry for 3-5 minutes, until tender crisp.

5   Add soy sauce, salt, and pepper; stir-fry 2 minutes longer.

6   Assembly: Place green beans onto a serving platter. Top with crunchy potato rounds. Serve immediately.

VARIATION

GREEN BEAN SALAD

Cut green beans into 2-inch pieces. Prepare recipe as directed in Steps 1-5. Place green beans and potatoes into a serving bowl; toss together. Serve hot or at room temperature.

Herbed Honey-Roasted Tomatoes

PAREVE I PASSOVER I GLUTEN-FREE I YIELDS 6-8 SERVINGS

INGREDIENTS

3-4 large firm tomatoes,
trimmed and halved crosswise

¼ cup extra light olive oil

2 Tbsp honey

6 cloves garlic
minced (about 3 tsp)

⅓ cup finely diced red onion

¼ cup chopped fresh basil
or 4 frozen basil cubes

1 tsp kosher salt

¼ tsp black pepper

sprigs of fresh herbs
(e.g., thyme, oregano, rosemary)

METHOD

1   Preheat oven to 400°F.
Coat a 9 x 13-inch glass or
ceramic dish with nonstick
cooking spray.

2   Arrange tomato halves in a single layer in prepared baking dish.

3   In a medium bowl, combine oil, honey, garlic, onion, basil, salt, and pepper; mix well.

4   Spoon mixture evenly over tomatoes; top with herbs. (Can be prepared ahead of time.)

5   Bake, uncovered, for 30-40 minutes (depending on size of tomatoes), until tomatoes are tender. Serve immediately.

VARIATION

CHERRY TOMATO RAMEKINS

Prepare mixture in Step 3 to form a dressing. Preheat oven to 400°F. Wash and dry 1-2 pints **cherry tomatoes;** cut tomatoes in half. Coat 6-8 ramekins with nonstick cooking spray. Place ⅓ cup tomatoes into each ramekin; top with dressing. Bake, uncovered, for 20-25 minutes.

Dilled Roasted Cauliflower and Broccoli

PAREVE I PASSOVER I GLUTEN-FREE I YIELDS 6-8 SERVINGS

INGREDIENTS

1 large cauliflower
trimmed, cut into 2-inch florets

1 large broccoli
trimmed, cut into 2-inch florets

1 tsp kosher salt

black pepper

2 Tbsp honey

2 tsp onion powder

¼ cup chopped fresh dill

3 Tbsp extra light olive oil

METHOD

1   Preheat oven to 400°F. Line a large rimmed baking sheet with parchment paper.

2   In a large bowl, combine all ingredients; mix well. Spread evenly onto prepared baking sheet.

3   Bake, uncovered, for 35-45 minutes, until cauliflower and broccoli are tender-crisp.

VARIATION

SHREDDED VEGGIE HASH

Preheat oven to 400°F. Using a food processor fitted with the shredding disc, shred broccoli and cauliflower. Transfer to a large rimmed baking sheet lined with parchment paper. Add remaining ingredients; toss well to combine. Bake, uncovered, for 30-35 minutes, until tender-crisp.

Peanut Butter Sweet Potatoes

PAREVE I GLUTEN-FREE I YIELDS 6-8 SERVINGS

INGREDIENTS

3-4 medium sweet potatoes
*scrubbed and thinly sliced
lengthwise into "steaks"
(do not peel)*

1 cup crunchy or smooth
peanut butter or Wow
butter

3 Tbsp honey

1 Tbsp extra light olive oil

½ cup salted peanuts

METHOD

1   Preheat oven to 350°F. Line
    a large rimmed baking sheet
    with parchment paper.

2   Arrange sweet potato
    "steaks" in a single layer on
    prepared baking sheet.

3   In a medium bowl, combine peanut butter with honey and oil; stir well to combine.

4   Spread 1-2 tablespoons peanut butter mixture onto each "steak." Top with crushed peanuts. Repeat with remaining ingredients.

5   Bake, uncovered, for 30-35 minutes, or until sweet potatoes are tender when pierced with a fork.

VARIATION

SWEET POTATO ROUNDS

Prepare recipe as directed, but slice each sweet potato into rounds. Use about 1 tablespoon of peanut butter mixture on each.

Steamed Broccoli With Ginger Topping

PAREVE I GLUTEN-FREE I YIELDS 6-8 SERVINGS

INGREDIENTS

1 head broccoli
trimmed, cut into florets

ASIAN TOPPING

2 Tbsp extra light olive oil

2 scallions
trimmed and thinly sliced

1½-2 tsp grated fresh
ginger

3 Tbsp soy sauce or tamari

4 cloves garlic
minced (about 2 tsp)

METHOD

1   Bring a large pot of water to
a boil. Add steamer basket;
add broccoli to steamer.
Steam for 5-7 minutes, until
tender-crisp. Remove from
heat; transfer to serving
platter.

2   Topping: In a large frying pan over medium heat, heat oil. Add scallions, ginger, soy sauce, and garlic; cook for 2-3 minutes. Add broccoli; stir to combine. Do not overcook or broccoli will become too soft.

3   Drizzle topping over broccoli; serve immediately.

VARIATION

GINGERY STEAMED CABBAGE

Instead of broccoli, use 1 medium **cabbage** (white or red), cut into 1-2-inch thick slices. Prepare recipe as directed.

Salted Baby Potatoes

PAREVE I PASSOVER I GLUTEN-FREE I YIELDS 4-6 SERVINGS

INGREDIENTS

2 cups kosher salt

1 pkg (1.5 lb/600 g)
baby potatoes
washed and scrubbed

fresh rosemary or thyme

2 Tbsp extra light olive oil

METHOD

1 In a large skillet, scatter salt evenly, creating a base. Heat on medium-high for about 5 minutes, until warm.

2 Arrange potatoes in a single layer on bed of salt, pressing lightly into salt. Cover with foil; cook on stovetop for 24-35 minutes or until potatoes are tender.

VARIATION

POTATO SKEWERS

Prepare recipe as directed. Using a short skewer, pierce 3-4 potatoes; place onto a serving platter. Repeat with remaining potatoes. Serve family style, on individual plates, or as an appetizer for a party.

3   Using tongs, remove potatoes from skillet; brush off excess salt. Transfer to a serving dish.

4   Top with fresh herbs; drizzle with oil. Cover with foil and shake dish to coat all sides. Keep covered for 5 minutes. Serve hot.

Hash Brown "Potato Kugel" Waffles

PAREVE/MEAT VARIATION I PASSOVER I GLUTEN-FREE I YIELDS 6 SERVINGS

INGREDIENTS

4 lb Yukon potatoes
peeled (about 8 medium)

1 large onion, chopped

1 egg

1 Tbsp kosher salt

¼ tsp black pepper

4 Tbsp extra light olive oil

1 tsp sweet paprika

METHOD

1 In a food processor fitted
   with the shredding disk,
   shred potatoes and onions,
   using medium pressure.
   Transfer vegetables to a
   large colander set in the sink
   or over a bowl; press firmly
   to drain excess liquid.

2 Transfer drained veggies to
   a large bowl. Add egg, salt,
   pepper, oil, and paprika.
   Mix well.

3   Turn on waffle maker; coat with nonstick cooking spray.

4   Spoon about ¾-cup potato mixture into waffle compartment; spread evenly. Cook until potatoes are browned on both sides. Add more nonstick cooking spray if needed. Cut each into quarters.

VARIATION

DELI HASH BROWN PIZZA

Prepare recipe as directed, but do not cut waffles into quarters. Place waffles on a large serving platter. Top with **1 lb sliced corned beef, 3 pickles,** trimmed and sliced, and a drizzle of **spicy mayo**. Serve immediately. Alternatively, serve on individual plates, dividing toppings evenly among them.

Great to serve as an appetizer or on Chanukah.

DESSERT

Double Chocolate Banana Cake

PAREVE I GLUTEN-FREE OPTION I FREEZES WELL I YIELDS 2 LOAVES

INGREDIENTS

2 eggs

1 cup brown sugar

½ cup vegetable oil

2 tsp pure vanilla extract

2 large, very ripe bananas
mashed

1¾ cups flour
(or gluten-free flour)

¼ cup cocoa powder

1 tsp baking soda

1 tsp baking powder

pinch salt

¾ cup orange juice or
apple juice

1½ cups mini chocolate
chips

METHOD

1   Preheat oven to 350°F. Coat
    2 (9 x 5-inch) loaf pans with
    nonstick cooking spray.

2   In a medium bowl, whisk
    together eggs, brown sugar,
    oil, and vanilla until light. Mix
    in mashed bananas.

3   Stir in flour, cocoa, baking soda, baking powder, and salt. Mix in juice; fold in chocolate chips.

4   Divide batter evenly between prepared loaf pans. Bake for 45-55 minutes, or until a wooden toothpick inserted into the center comes out dry.

VARIATION

DOUBLE CHOCOLATE MUFFINS

Prepare recipe as directed, using large and small muffin tins coated with nonstick cooking spray. Scoop batter into each compartment. Bake large muffins for 18-25 minutes and small muffins for 15-18 minutes, until set.

Chocolate Covered Chickpeas

PAREVE I GLUTEN-FREE I FREEZES WELL I YIELDS 6 SERVINGS

INGREDIENTS

1 bag (9 oz/ 255 g)
chocolate chips

2 cups roasted salted
chickpeas (store-bought)
divided

METHOD

1   Line a rimmed baking sheet with parchment paper.

2   Pour about 1-inch water into a saucepan. Bring to a boil; reduce heat to a simmer.

3   Place chocolate into a large, dry, heatproof bowl wider than the saucepan. Place bowl over simmering water. Melt chocolate, stirring often.

4   Stir about half the chickpeas into melted chocolate. Pour chocolate mixture onto prepared baking sheet; spread evenly. Sprinkle with remaining chickpeas; pressing gently into chocolate.

5   Refrigerate for 45 minutes, until chocolate is set. Break into small, irregular pieces. Store in an airtight container.

VARIATION

FLAVORED CHOCOLATE CHICKPEAS

Prepare recipe as directed, using various **flavored chickpeas** (e.g., cinnamon sugar, sweet chili).

Strawberry Almond Tart

PAREVE I GLUTEN-FREE OPTION I FREEZES WELL I YIELD 8-10 SERVINGS

INGREDIENTS

1 cup flour
(or gluten-free flour)

1 cup almond flour

½ cup sugar

1 tsp salt

⅔ cup vegetable oil

1 Tbsp water

FILLING

1 lb strawberries
quartered (fresh or frozen)

2 Tbsp sugar

2 Tbsp flour

1 tsp lemon juice

¼ cup sliced almonds

ground cinnamon
for sprinkling

METHOD

1   Preheat oven to 350°F. Line a 9- or 10-inch round or ceramic tart pan with parchment paper; coat the sides with nonstick cooking spray

2   In a medium bowl, combine flour, almond flour, sugar, salt, oil, and water; mix well to form a dough. Reserve ½ cup for topping. Place remaining dough into prepared tart pan, pressing down and up the sides to form a crust.

3   Filling: In a second bowl, combine strawberries
    with sugar, flour, lemon juice, and almonds;
    mix well. Spoon into crust. Crumble reserved
    dough; sprinkle crumbs and cinnamon over
    filling.

4   Bake for 45-50 minutes, until golden.

VARIATION

PEACH CRISPS

Prepare recipe as directed using 6
peaches, peeled and cut into chunks.
You can use mini tart pans for a
different presentation. Bake for 30-
40 minutes. This recipe also works
well in a rectangular tart pan.

Peanut Butter Chocolate Popcorn

PAREVE I GLUTEN-FREE I FREEZES WELL I YIELDS 10-12 SERVINGS

INGREDIENTS

1 bag *(9 oz/ 255 g)* **chocolate chips**

½ cup peanut butter

8 cups popped popcorn
salted or unsalted

METHOD

1   Line the bottom of a springform pan with parchment paper. Coat the sides with nonstick cooking spray.

2   In a large pot, combine chocolate and peanut butter. Heat over medium-low until melted.

3   Fold in popcorn, coating all sides with chocolate mixture.

4   Spoon popcorn evenly into springform pan.

5   Refrigerate or freeze for 20-30 minutes, until set. If frozen, take out 5 minutes before serving. Serve chilled. Cut into slices.

VARIATION

POPCORN BARK

Prepare recipe as directed in Steps 2 and 3. Spread mixture evenly onto parchment-lined baking sheet. Refrigerate or freeze for 20-30 minutes, until set. Break into irregular pieces.

Low-Fat Ginger Biscotti

PAREVE I GLUTEN-FREE OPTION I FREEZES WELL I YIELDS 2-3 DOZEN

INGREDIENTS

½ cup vegetable oil

2 eggs

½ cup pure maple syrup

2 tsp pure vanilla extract

1 Tbsp molasses

2⅓ cups flour
(or gluten-free flour)

1 tsp baking soda

pinch salt

1½ tsp ground cinnamon

1½ tsp ground ginger

½ tsp ground cloves

1½ cups white chocolate chips

METHOD

1   Preheat oven to 350°F. Line a rimmed baking sheet with parchment paper.

2   In a large mixing bowl, whisk together oil, eggs, maple syrup, vanilla, and molasses until well blended. Stir in flour, baking soda, salt, cinnamon, ginger, and cloves, making a sticky, thick batter. Fold in white chocolate chips.

3　Transfer dough to prepared baking sheet and shape into two long, narrow logs (about 1½-inches wide). Bake for 25 minutes, or until firm.

4　Reduce oven temperature to 300°F. Using a serrated knife, cut logs into slices about ¾-inch thick. Return slices to baking sheet, cut-side up. Bake for 15-25 minutes, until golden. (For crunchier biscotti, bake for 25 minutes; for a chewier texture, bake for 15-20 minutes).

VARIATION

GINGER BERRY CUPS

Follow recipe as directed. Place biscotti into a resealable plastic bag. Using a meat hammer or wooden spoon, smash biscotti into crumbs. Fill 4-6 parfait cups with an assortment of **berries** (e.g., blueberries, strawberries); top each with 2-3 tablespoons crushed biscotti.

Mint Chocolate Chip Cookies

PAREVE/DAIRY OPTION I GLUTEN-FREE OPTION
FREEZES WELL I YIELDS ABOUT 15 LARGE COOKIES

INGREDIENTS

¾ cup vegetable oil

1 cup white sugar

½ cup brown sugar

2 eggs

2 tsp pure mint extract

4 tsp minced fresh mint

1¾ cups flour
(or gluten-free flour)

1 tsp baking soda

pinch salt

2 cups chocolate chips or
chopped chocolate

METHOD

1   In a large bowl, combine oil,
sugars, eggs, mint extract,
and mint. Mix until well
blended, 1-2 minutes. (You
can use an electric mixer.)

2   Add flour, baking soda, and
salt, mix just until combined.
Stir in chocolate chips.

3   Cover; refrigerate for 1 hour or overnight.

4   Preheat oven to 350°F. Line two baking
    sheets with parchment paper.

5   Using a large cookie scoop, drop golf-ball-
    size mounds of dough 2 inches apart onto
    prepared baking sheets.

6   Bake for 13-15 minutes, until set. Let cool.

VARIATION

ICE CREAM SANDWICHES

Prepare recipe as directed. Spoon
about ⅓-cup **ice cream**, pareve or
dairy, onto a cookie; top with a second
cookie. These can be prepared in
advance and kept in the freezer.

Great for a party or Shavuot.

Espresso Chocolate Chip Cookies

PAREVE I GLUTEN-FREE OPTION I FREEZES WELL
YIELDS 15 ABOUT LARGE COOKIES

INGREDIENTS

1 cup vegetable oil

1 cup brown sugar

½ cup white sugar

2 eggs

1 tsp pure vanilla extract

3 Tbsp granulated coffee
dissolved in 1 Tbsp hot
water

2 cups flour
(or gluten-free flour)

1 tsp baking soda

1 tsp baking powder

1 bag (9 oz) dark
chocolate chips

METHOD

1 In a large bowl, combine oil,
   sugars, eggs, vanilla, and
   coffee mixture. Use a spoon
   to mix until well blended,
   1-2 minutes. (You can use an
   electric mixer.)

2 Add flour, baking soda, and
   baking powder; mix just until
   combined. Stir in chocolate
   chips.

3   Cover; refrigerate for 1 hour or overnight.

4   Preheat oven to 350°F. Line two baking
    sheets with parchment paper.

5   Using a large cookie scoop, drop golf-ball-
    size mounds of dough 2 inches apart onto
    prepared baking sheets.

6   Bake for 13-15 minutes,
    until set. Let cool.

VARIATION

MINI ESPRESSO COOKIES

Prepare recipe through Step 4. Using
a mini cookie scoop or a tablespoon,
scoop batter onto prepared baking
sheet. Bake for 7-9 minutes.

Black and White Moist Chocolate Cake

PAREVE I GLUTEN-FREE OPTION I FREEZES WELL I YIELDS 10-12 SERVINGS

INGREDIENTS

2 cups flour
(or gluten-free flour)

1½ cups sugar

¾ cup cocoa powder

1 tsp baking soda

2 tsp baking powder

pinch salt

1 cup orange juice

½ cup vegetable oil

2 eggs

2 tsp pure vanilla extract

1 cup boiling water

TOPPING

1 cup powdered sugar

4 Tbsp cocoa powder

7-8 tsp water

1 cup mixed white
and dark chocolate chips
for topping

METHOD

1   Preheat oven to 350°F. Coat a Bundt pan with nonstick cooking spray.

2   In the bowl of an electric mixer, on low speed, combine flour, sugar, cocoa, baking powder, baking soda and salt. Mix until combined.

3   Add juice, oil, eggs, and vanilla; beat on medium speed until well blended, about 1 minute. Carefully add boiling water; mix until smooth.

4   Pour batter into prepared pan. Bake for 50-55 minutes, or until set.

5   Meanwhile, in a small bowl, combine powdered sugar, cocoa, and water; mix until thick.

6   Cool cake completely. Spread cake with icing; top with white and dark chocolate chips.

VARIATION

MINI CAKES

Prepare recipe as directed. Pour batter into 8-10 small Bundt cake pans until ¾-full, or use donut molds. Bake for about 30 minutes. You can leave them plain, top with glaze and chocolate chips, or drizzle with chocolate.

Classic Fruit Flan

DAIRY I GLUTEN-FREE OPTION I YIELDS 8-10 SERVINGS

INGREDIENTS

DOUGH

1½ cups flour
(or gluten-free flour)

¼ cup sugar

¾ cup vegetable oil

1½ Tbsp vinegar

LEMON FILLING

5 large eggs

2 Tbsp lemon zest

⅓ cup honey

½ cup fresh lemon juice

2 tsp pure vanilla extract

6 Tbsp vegetable oil or
coconut oil

FRUIT

4 cups assorted fruit
halved, sliced, or cubed
(e.g., strawberries, blueberries,
kiwi, mango, etc.)

METHOD

1   Preheat oven to 375°F.
Lightly coat a 10-inch
flan pan or pie plate with
removable bottom with
nonstick cooking spray.

2   Dough: In a large bowl,
combine flour, sugar, oil, and
vinegar; mix to make a soft
dough.

3   Press dough evenly
against bottom and sides
of prepared pan. Bake,
uncovered, for 35-40
minutes, until golden.

4 Meanwhile, combine all filling ingredients in a small pot. Heat mixture, stirring continuously (so as not to curdle the eggs), until the lemon mixture becomes thick. Let cool slightly. Using a mesh bag or strainer, strain filling until smooth. Let cool completely. Refrigerate until ready to serve

5 Shortly before serving, pour lemon filling into pie crust. Arrange fruit over filling. Serve immediately.

VARIATION

LEMON PARFAIT

Prepare lemon filling as directed in Step 4. Spoon filling into parfait glasses; top with cubes of fresh fruit.

The Blue Cake

PAREVE I GLUTEN-FREE OPTION I FREEZES WELL I YIELDS 12 SERVINGS

INGREDIENTS

3 eggs

1¼ sugar

1¼ cup vegetable oil

1 tsp pure vanilla extract

1½ cup orange juice

2½ cups flour
(or gluten-free flour)

1 tsp baking powder

1½ tsp baking soda

pinch kosher salt

ICING

1 cup powdered sugar

2 Tbsp water

¼ tsp blue food coloring

METHOD

1   Preheat oven to 350°F. Coat
    a Bundt pan with nonstick
    cooking spray.

2   In the bowl of an electric mixer on medium speed, combine eggs, sugar, oil, and vanilla; mix well. Add juice, beating to combine.

3   On low speed, beat in flour, baking powder, baking soda, and salt.

4   Pour batter into prepared pan. Bake for 50-55 minutes, or until set. Cool completely.

5   Icing: In a small bowl, combine powdered sugar, water, and food coloring; mix until thickened. Spread icing over cake.

VARIATION

COLORFUL CAKES

Prepare recipe as directed, preparing the icing in small batches using various colors of **food coloring**. Great to serve for a party.

Coconut Chocolate Tart

PAREVE I PASSOVER I GLUTEN-FREE I FREEZES WELL I YIELDS 10 SERVINGS

INGREDIENTS

CRUST

2 large egg whites

3 cups sweetened shredded coconut
plus more for garnish

⅓ cup sugar

3 Tbsp oil or coconut oil

pinch salt

GANACHE FILLING

1¼ cups nondairy whipping cream

1 bag (9 oz) chocolate chips

METHOD

1   Preheat oven to 350°F. Coat bottom and sides of a 9- or 10-inch glass pie plate (or a tart pan with removable bottom) with nonstick cooking spray.

2   Crust: Combine eggs, coconut, sugar, oil, and salt; stir to combine. Pat evenly into bottom and up the sides of prepared pan to form a crust.

3   Bake 20-25 minutes, or until crust is golden and set. Let cool.

4   Ganache Filling: In a medium saucepan, bring cream to a boil over medium-high heat. Transfer to a bowl. Add chocolate; stir until melted.

5   Pour ganache into cooled crust. Let set for 10 minutes. Sprinkle with additional coconut. Refrigerate for 4 hours or overnight. Serve chilled.

VARIATION

RECTANGULAR COCONUT TART

Prepare recipe as directed using a removable-bottom rectangular tart pan or a 9 x 13 inch glass baking dish. Omit coconut topping.

Coconut Strawberry Shortcake

PAREVE I GLUTEN-FREE OPTION I FREEZES WELL I YIELDS 10-12 SERVINGS

INGREDIENTS

1¼ cups vegetable oil

1⅓ cups sugar

3 eggs

2 tsp pure vanilla extract

pinch kosher salt

1½ cups orange juice

2½ cups flour
(or gluten-free flour)

1 tsp baking powder

1½ tsp baking soda

1 container (255 g)
coconut whipping cream

2 lb strawberries
trimmed and sliced

METHOD

1 Preheat oven to 350°F. Line bottom of a springform pan with parchment paper; coat the sides with nonstick cooking spray.

2 In a large bowl, or in the bowl of an electric mixer, combine oil, sugar, eggs, vanilla, and salt. Add orange juice; mix until light in color. Add flour, baking powder, and baking soda, beating until just combined.

3   Pour batter into prepared pan. Bake, uncovered, for 45-50 minutes, until set. Cool completely.

4   Assembly: Cut cake horizontally into two layers. Place one cake layer onto a serving platter. Top with whipped cream and sliced strawberries. Top with second cake layer; spread with whipped cream. Top with strawberries. If you have enough whipped cream, spread over cake sides.

VARIATION

BERRY CUPS

Prepare cake as directed. Let cool. Place a dollop of coconut whipped cream into individual cups. Cut cake into 2-inch chunks; add to cups. Top with ½ cup **berries** (e.g., blueberries, strawberries). Repeat for a tiered presentation, if desired.

Olive Oil Salted Brownies

PAREVE I GLUTEN-FREE OPTION I FREEZES WELL I YIELDS 8-10 SERVINGS

INGREDIENTS

¼ cup extra light olive oil

1 bag (9 oz)
chocolate chips

¾ cup sugar

2 eggs

1 tsp pure vanilla extract

¼ cup flour
(or gluten-free flour)

1 tsp instant coffee granules

1 tsp baking powder

coarse sea salt, for
sprinkling

METHOD

1 Preheat oven to 350°F. Line
an 8 x 8-inch baking pan
with parchment paper.

2 In a heatproof bowl, combine
chocolate and oil. Melt in the
microwave or in a double
broiler; let cool slightly.

3 Stir in sugar, eggs, and
vanilla; mix until combined.
Mix in flour, coffee, and
baking powder.

4   Pour into prepared baking pan; sprinkle with
    sea salt.

5   Bake, uncovered, for 30-35 minutes, until
    brownie is set but still gooey in center.

6   Sprinkle with a dash more sea salt. Cut into
    squares.

VARIATION

SALTED BROWNIE CAKE

Prepare recipe as directed, using
a 9- or 10-inch round baking dish
and coating the bottom and sides
with nonstick cooking spray. Pour
into prepared pan; bake as directed.
Sprinkle with a dash more sea salt.
Cut into slices to serve.

Rose Petal Apple Tart

PAREVE I GLUTEN-FREE OPTION I YIELDS 10 SERVINGS

INGREDIENTS

DOUGH

1½ cups flour
(or gluten-free flour)

¼ cup brown sugar

1 tsp ground cinnamon

¾ cup vegetable oil

1½ Tbsp vinegar

FILLING

5-6 apples
thinly sliced on a mandoline (do not peel)

3 Tbsp brown sugar

2 tsp ground cinnamon

2 tsp fresh lemon juice

METHOD

1 Preheat oven to 375°F. Lightly coat a 9- or 10-inch flan pan or pie plate with removable bottom with nonstick cooking spray.

2 In a large bowl, combine flour, brown sugar, cinnamon, oil, and vinegar; mix to make a soft dough.

3 Press dough evenly against bottom and sides of prepared pan.

4. In a medium bowl, combine sliced apples with brown sugar, cinnamon, and lemon juice; gently mix well.

5. Starting at the outer edge of pan, place apple slices slightly on an angle to form a circle, making sure to overlap the apples. Repeat with additional rows, working your way toward center.

6. Place additional apples in any gaps (apples should be tightly packed). Pour on any remaining liquid in apple bowl.

7. Bake for 45-50 minutes.

VARIATION

APPLE CRISPS

Preheat oven to 375°F. Peel, core, and cut apples into large chunks. Place into large bowl; mix with brown sugar, cinnamon, and lemon juice. Place into individual ramekins. Bake, uncovered, for 25-30 minutes. Serve hot or at room temperature.

Afternoon Snack Bars

PAREVE I GLUTEN-FREE OPTION I FREEZES WELL I YIELDS ABOUT 16 BARS

INGREDIENTS

2 cups large flaked oats
(gluten-free or regular)

½ cup nut butter or Wow butter

½ cup honey

pinch salt

2 tsp pure vanilla extract

MIX-IN OPTIONS

½ cup mini chocolate chips

½ cup dried cranberries or raisins

½ cup pumpkin seeds

½ cup peanuts

½ cup mini chocolate lentils

METHOD

1   Line a rimmed baking sheet with parchment paper.

2   In a medium bowl, combine oats with nut butter, honey, salt, and vanilla. Add up to 1 cup mix-in option of choice.

3   Place batter into an 8 x 8-inch baking dish
     lined with parchment paper; flatten by
     covering with a second piece of parchment
     paper and pressing down.

4   Let set in the refrigerator for 30 minutes. Cut
     into long strips. Store in an airtight container
     in the refrigerator or freezer.

VARIATION

GRANOLA BALLS

Prepare Steps 1 and 2 as directed.
Using a large cookie scoop, scoop
mixture onto prepared baking sheet.
Refrigerate for 30 minutes. Store in
an airtight container in the refrigerator
or freezer.

Cayenne-Lime Mango and Watermelon

PAREVE | PASSOVER | GLUTEN-FREE | YIELDS 4-6 SERVINGS

INGREDIENTS

2 mangoes
*peeled, pitted,
and cut into thin strips*

⅓ watermelon
cut into thin wedges

zest and juice of 4 limes

pinch cayenne pepper
optional

METHOD

1   Arrange mango and
    watermelon on a serving
    platter.

2   Sprinkle with lime zest;
    drizzle with lime juice. Add a
    dash of cayenne, if using.

VARIATION

LIME ZEST FRUIT CUPS

Cut mango and watermelon into chunks. Plate in individual dessert cups. Top with **pomegranate seeds** or other fruit (e.g., **strawberries, blueberries**, etc.). Drizzle with zest, juice, and a sprinkle of cayenne.

Dragon Fruit Salad

PAREVE I GLUTEN-FREE I YIELDS 4 SERVINGS

INGREDIENTS

2 dragon fruit

1 pint strawberries
trimmed, halved lengthwise

1 pint blueberries

1 lemon

2 tsp honey

mint leaves
for garnish

METHOD

1   Cut the dragon fruit in half lengthwise. Using a melon baller, scoop the flesh into pretty balls.

2   Place into a serving bowl; add strawberries and blueberries. Drizzle with lemon juice and honey.

3   Garnish with fresh mint.

VARIATION

DRAGON FRUIT SKEWERS

Prepare recipe as directed, omitting blueberries. Thread 2-4 pieces of fruit onto skewers. Drizzle skewered fruit with lemon juice and honey. If you prefer, cut the dragon fruit into chunks rather than forming balls.

Candied Marshmallow Lollipops

PAREVE I GLUTEN-FREE I PASSOVER I FREEZES WELL I YIELDS 10-15 LOLLYPOPS

INGREDIENTS

1 bag (12 oz) jumbo
marshmallows

1 bag (9 oz) chocolate chips

¾ cup colored sprinkles

10-15 lollypop sticks

METHOD

1 Line a rimmed baking sheet
   with parchment paper.

2 Pour about 1-inch water into
   saucepan. Bring to a boil;
   reduce heat to a simmer.

3   Place chocolate chips into a large, dry, heatproof bowl wider than the saucepan. Place bowl over saucepan. Melt chocolate, stirring often.

4   Place sprinkles into a small shallow bowl. Using lollypop sticks, pierce each marshmallow half way through. Dunk into melted chocolate and then into sprinkles. Place onto prepared baking sheet.

5   Chill or freeze for 30 minutes, or until chocolate has set.

VARIATION

MARSHMALLOW CAKE

Line the bottom of a springform pan with parchment paper. Prepare chocolate as directed in Steps 2 and 3. Reserve ¼ cup chocolate. Spread remaining chocolate evenly into prepared pan. Arrange 1 bag of large or mini marshmallows on melted chocolate, arranging in a circular pattern. Drizzle with reserved chocolate; sprinkle with sprinkles. Chill until serving time. Unmold onto a serving platter.

NUTRITIONAL INFORMATION

- The nutritional analysis was calculated using data from ESHA (The Food Processor SQL Edition 10.14.2) and, when necessary, manufacturers' food labels.

- Values given for each recipe are per serving unless stated otherwise

- When there is a choice of ingredients, the first ingredient was analyzed. The analysis does not include optional ingredients or those with no specified amounts.

- The smaller measure of an ingredient was analyzed when a range is given (e.g., ¼ cup was analyzed when a recipe calls for ¼-⅓ cup).

- The nutrient values have been rounded off for carbohydrates, fiber, fat, calories, protein, cholesterol, sodium, potassium, iron, calcium, and phosphorus.

- The phosphorus content included in the analysis is helpful for people with medical problems, including kidney disease.

- When milk is called for, the recipe was analyzed using 1% milk, unless otherwise indicated.

- When eggs are called for, the recipe was analyzed using large eggs.

- Garnishes were not calculated, unless a specific amount is indicated.

- A serving of at least 2 grams fiber is considered a moderate source, 4 grams is a high source, and 6 grams is considered a very high source fiber.

- When cheese is called for, the recipe was analyzed using lower fat or reduced fat cheeses, unless otherwise indicated.

- When sour cream or yogurt is called for, the recipe was analyzed using lower fat versions, unless otherwise indicated.

- Specific measurements of salt were included in the analysis (e.g., 1 tsp salt). When a recipe does not give a specific measurement (e.g., salt to taste), then salt was not included in the analysis. To reduce sodium content, choose low-sodium or salt-free products. Note that sodium content varies by brand of soy or tamari sauce; the sodium content of your dish may vary from the amount listed in this directory.

- To keep your recipes gluten-free, use gluten-free soy sauce or tamari.

- To keep your recipes dairy-free, use rice, soy, unsweetened almond, or coconut milk.

APPETIZERS

Corned Beef-Topped Eggplant p. 14
Calories: 460 kcal
Carbs: 21 g (15 g sugar, 5 g fiber)
Protein: 33 g
Fat: 27.8 g (8.6 g saturated)
Cholesterol: 98 mg
Potassium: 567 mg
Calcium: 40 mg
Sodium: 1311 mg
Iron: 3 mg

Turkey-Wrapped Enoki Mushrooms p. 16
Calories: 199 kcal
Carbs: 19 g (12 g sugar, 3 g of fiber)
Protein: 23 g
Fat: 4.5 g (0.7 g saturated)
Cholesterol: 41 mg
Potassium: 505 mg
Calcium: 8 mg
Sodium: 1001 mg
Iron: 2 mg

Sesame Seed Rice Balls p. 18
Calories: 74 kcal
Carbs: 13 g (0 g sugar, 1 g fiber)
Protein: 2 g
Fat: 1.6 g (0.2 g saturated)
Cholesterol: 0 mg
Potassium: 26 mg
Calcium: 32 mg
Sodium: 162 mg
Iron: <1 mg

Deli-Wrapped Squash Bites p. 20
Calories: 55 kcal
Carbs: 9 g (4 g sugar, 1 g fiber)
Protein: 2 g
Fat: 1.8 g (0.7 g saturated)
Cholesterol: 7 mg
Potassium: 183 mg
Calcium: 27 mg
Sodium: 119 mg
Iron: <1 mg

Crunchy Chicken Kale Salad p. 22
Calories: 754 kcal
Carbs: 53 g (17 g sugar, 11 g fiber)
Protein: 33 g
Fat: 51.2 g (9.7 g saturated)
Cholesterol: 68 mg
Potassium: 1459 mg
Calcium: 221 mg
Sodium: 397 mg
Iron: 4 mg

Deli Egg Rolls p. 24
Calories: 450 kcal
Carbs: 30 g (7 g sugar, 3 g fiber)
Protein: 26 g
Fat: 25.9 g (7.2 g saturated)
Cholesterol: 95 mg
Potassium: 409 mg
Calcium: 31 mg
Sodium: 1673 mg
Iron: 3 mg

Corned Beef Biscotti p. 26
Calories: 240 kcal
Carbs: 32 g (4 g sugar, 1 g fiber)
Protein: 9 g
Fat: 7.9 g (1.9 g saturated)
Cholesterol: 31 mg
Potassium: 83 mg
Calcium: 17 mg
Sodium: 217 mg
Iron: 2 mg

Cucumber Roll Ups p. 28
Calories: 174 kcal
Carbs: 10 g (4 g sugar, 3 g fiber)
Protein: 16 g
Fat: 8.0 g (1.9 g saturated)
Cholesterol: 192 mg
Potassium: 356 mg
Calcium: 167 mg
Sodium: 507 mg
Iron: 4 mg

Zaatar Avocado p. 30
Calories: 114 kcal
Carbs: 6 g (0 g sugar, 5 g fiber)
Protein: 1 g
Fat: 10.5 g (1.5 g saturated)
Cholesterol: 0 mg
Potassium: 345 mg
Calcium: 9 mg
Sodium: 5 mg
Iron: 0 mg

Cute Baguette Cups p. 32
Calories: 158 kcal
Carbs: 33 g (7 g sugar, 5 g fiber)
Protein: 6 g
Fat: 0.5 g (0.1 g saturated)
Cholesterol: 0 mg
Potassium: 555 mg
Calcium: 55 mg
Sodium: 242 mg
Iron: 4 mg

Lemon Herbed Bone Marrow p. 34
Calories: 1050 kcal
Carbs: 22 g (7 g sugar, 1 g fiber)
Protein: 10 g
Fat: 103 g (1 g saturated)
Cholesterol: 0 mg
Potassium: 44 mg
Calcium: 17 mg
Sodium: 35 mg
Iron: 5 mg

Dill Pickle Football Wings p. 36
Calories: 442 kcal
Carbs: 7 g (6 g sugar, 1 g fiber)
Protein: 35 g
Fat: 30.0 g (7.6 g saturated)
Cholesterol: 218 mg
Potassium: 399 mg
Calcium: 24 mg
Sodium: 426 mg
Iron: 1 mg

SOUPS

Healing Celery Soup p. 40
Calories: 119 kcal
Carbs: 18 g (4 g sugar, 4 g fiber)
Protein: 3 g
Fat: 4.9 g (0.7 g saturated)
Cholesterol: 0 mg
Potassium: 324 mg
Calcium: 88 mg
Sodium: 918 mg
(or 118 mg if salt to taste)
Iron: <1 mg

Sweet Potato Pear Soup p. 42

Calories: 109 kcal

Carbs: 19 g (7 g sugar, 4 g fiber)

Protein: 2 g

Fat: 3.7 g (0.5 g saturated)

Cholesterol: 0 mg

Potassium: 310 mg

Calcium: 34 mg

Sodium: 46 mg

Iron: <1 mg

Crunchy Soup Toppings p. 44

Carbs: 11 g (0 g sugar, 0 g fiber)

Protein: 2 g

Fat: 4.7 g (0.7 g saturated)

Cholesterol: 0 mg

Potassium: 10 mg

Calcium: 2 mg

Sodium: 342 mg

Iron: 0 mg

Spiralized Noodle Soup p. 48

Calories: 116 kcal

Carbs: 17 g (6 g sugar, 3 g fiber)

Protein: 4 g

Fat: 3.8 g (0.6 g saturated)

Cholesterol: 0 mg

Potassium: 424 mg

Calcium: 41 mg

Sodium: 822 mg

Iron: <1 mg

Chunky Mushroom Soup p.46

Calories: 82 kcal

Carbs: 10 g (4 g sugar, 3 g fiber)

Protein: 4 g

Fat: 3.9 g (0.6 g saturated)

Cholesterol: 0 mg

Potassium: 430 mg

Calcium: 27 mg

Sodium: 948 mg

Iron: 1 mg

Healthy Tomato Lentil Soup p. 50

Calories: 164 kcal

Carbs: 32 g (7 g sugar, 6 g fiber)

Protein: 10 g

Fat: 0.6 g (0.1 g saturated)

Cholesterol: 0 mg

Potassium: 685 mg

Calcium: 54 mg

Sodium: 699 mg

Iron: 3 mg

Vegetarian Vegetable Quinoa Soup p. 52

Calories: 218 kcal (163 kcal)

Carbs: 34 g (7 g sugar, 5 g fiber)-26 g (5 g sugar, 4 g fiber)

Protein: 6 g (protein 5 g)

Fat: 6.6 g (0.9 g saturated) (5.0 g (0.7 g saturated)

Cholesterol: 0 mg

Potassium: 499 mg (374 mg)

Calcium: 53 mg (40 mg)

Sodium: 713 mg (534 mg)

Iron: 2 mg (1 mg)

Broccoli Soup with Caramelized Leeks p. 54

Calories: 145 kcal

Carbs: 26 g (10 g sugar, 4 g fiber)

Protein: 4 g

Fat: 4.1 g (0.6 g saturated)

Cholesterol: 0 mg

Potassium: 422 mg

Calcium: 112 mg

Sodium: 528 mg

Iron: 3 mg

Roasted Kabocha Squash Soup p. 56

Calories: 87 kcal

Carbs: 13 g (6 g sugar, 2 g fiber)

Protein: 2 g

Fat: 3.6 g (0.5 g saturated)

Cholesterol: 0 mg

Potassium: 40 mg

Calcium: 39 mg

Sodium: 8 mg

Iron: <1 mg

Dinner Steak Soup p. 58

Calories: 346 kcal

Carbs: 19 g (3 g sugar, 4 g fiber)

Protein: 35 g

Fat: 14.0 g (4.7 g saturated)

Cholesterol: 96 mg

Potassium: 692 mg

Calcium: 55 mg

Sodium: 617 mg

Iron: 5 mg

SALADS

Simply Sweet Mini Pepper Salad p. 62

Calories: 168 kcal

Carbs: 13 g (9 g sugar, 3 g fiber)

Protein: 2 g

Fat: 12.9 g (1.8 g saturated)

Cholesterol: 0 mg

Potassium: 312 mg

Calcium: 17 mg

Sodium: 28 mg

Iron: <1 mg

Pea Shoot Salad p. 64

Calories: 268 kcal

Carbs: 38 g (30 g sugar, 4 g fiber)

Protein: 4 g

Fat: 12.8 g (1.8 g saturated)

Cholesterol: 0 mg

Potassium: 77 mg

Calcium: 49 mg

Sodium: 429 mg

Iron: 2 mg

Fresh Herb Granola Salad p. 66

Calories: 319 kcal

Carbs: 34 g (19 g sugar, 5 g fiber)

Protein: 5 g

Fat: 20.6 g (2.7 g saturated)

Cholesterol: 0 mg

Potassium: 391 mg

Calcium: 71 mg

Sodium: 47 mg

Iron: 2 mg

Avocado Lentil Salad p. 68

Calories: 545 kcal

Carbs: 54 g (6 g sugar, 23 g fiber)

Protein: 22 g

Fat: 30.1 g (4.2 g saturated)

Cholesterol: 0 mg

Potassium: 1292 mg

Calcium: 68 mg

Sodium: 1111 mg

Iron: 8 mg

Panko-Topped Kale Salad p. 70

Calories: 261 kcal

Carbs: 15 g (6 g sugar, 1 g fiber)

Protein: 3 g

Fat: 22.4 g (3.1 g saturated)

Cholesterol: 0 mg
Potassium: 103 mg
Calcium: 46 mg
Sodium: 174 mg
Iron: <1 mg

Black and White Avocado Salad p. 72

Calories: 216 kcal
Carbs: 15 g (1 g sugar, 7 g fiber)
Protein: 5 g
Fat: 18.8 g (3.4 g saturated)
Cholesterol: 0 mg
Potassium: 87 mg
Calcium: 54 mg
Sodium: 2 mg
Iron: 2 mg

Shredded Kale and Brussels Sprouts Salad p. 74

Calories: 318 kcal
Carbs: 25 g (13 g sugar, 5 g fiber)
Protein: 6 g
Fat: 24.1 g (3.1 g saturated)
Cholesterol: 0 mg
Potassium: 447 mg
Calcium: 90 mg
Sodium: 143 mg
Iron: 2 mg

Baby Romaine Halves With Lemon Dressing p. 76

Calories: 228 kcal
Carbs: 26 g (15 g sugar, 9 g fiber)
Protein: 6 g
Fat: 14.0 g (2.0 g saturated)
Cholesterol: 0 mg
Potassium: 1052 mg
Calcium: 141 mg
Sodium: 728 mg
Iron: 4 mg

Pretty Brussels Sprouts Salad p. 78

Calories: 375 kcal
Carbs: 33 g (19 g sugar, 6 g fiber)
Protein: 7 g
Fat: 27.3 g (4.4 g saturated)
Cholesterol: 0 mg
Potassium: 644 mg
Calcium: 76 mg
Sodium: 536 mg
Iron: 3 mg

Rainbow Bright Salad p. 80

Calories: 248 kcal
Carbs: 20 g (12 g sugar, 4 g fiber)
Protein: 4 g
Fat: 18.4 g (2.3 g saturated)
Cholesterol: 0 mg
Potassium: 353 mg
Calcium: 65 mg
Sodium: 117 mg
Iron: 1 mg

Baked Mini Falafel Ball Salad p. 82

Calories: 293 kcal
Carbs: 23 g (7 g sugar, 5 g fiber)
Protein: 8 g
Fat: 19.5 g (2.9 g saturated)
Cholesterol: 47 mg
Potassium: 382 mg
Calcium: 105 mg
Sodium: 394 mg
Iron: 2 mg

Three-Toned Cabbage Salad p. 84

Calories: 292 kcal
Carbs: 23 g (13 g sugar, 5 g fiber)
Protein: 7 g
Fat: 21.6 g (2.8 g saturated)
Cholesterol: 0 mg
Potassium: 495 mg
Calcium: 171 mg
Sodium: 1000 mg (or 640 mg if salt to taste)
Iron: 3 mg

Hemp Heart Cucumber Salad p. 86

Calories: 337 kcal
Carbs: 12 g (6 g sugar, 5 g fiber)
Protein: 12 g
Fat: 27.6 g (3.6 g saturated)
Cholesterol: 0 mg
Potassium: 494 mg
Calcium: 79 mg
Sodium: 373 mg
Iron: 5 mg

High-Fiber Salad Topper p. 88
per ¼ cup serving

Calories: 133 kcal
Carbs: 10 g (2 g sugar, 3 g fiber)

Protein: 4 g
Fat: 9.2 g (2.8 g saturated)
Cholesterol: 0 mg
Potassium: 79 mg
Calcium: 43 mg
Sodium: 2 mg
Iron: 1 mg

FISH

Hawaiian Poke Bowl p. 92

Calories: 634 kcal
Carbs: 109 g (8 g sugar, 7 g fiber)
Protein: 16 g
Fat: 14.3 g (1.9 g saturated)
Cholesterol: 9 mg
Potassium: 518 mg
Calcium: 46 mg
Sodium: 889 mg
Iron: 4 mg

Honey Mustard Pretzel Bites p. 94

Calories: 222 kcal
Carbs: 19 g (9 g sugar, 1 g fiber)
Protein: 10 g
Fat: 9.2 g (1.4 g saturated)
Cholesterol: 20 mg
Potassium: 194 mg
Calcium: 10 mg
Sodium: 841 mg
Iron: <1 mg

French Fried Onion Salmon p. 96

Calories: 322 kcal
Carbs: 12 g (6 g sugar, 0 g fiber)
Protein: 32 g
Fat: 15.7 g (3.2 g saturated)
Cholesterol: 70 mg
Potassium: 564 mg
Calcium: 22 mg
Sodium: 202 mg
Iron: <1 mg

Lemon Herbed Salmon Rolls With Asparagus p. 98

Calories: 415 kcal
Carbs: 9 g (4 g sugar, 4 g fiber)
Protein: 39 g

Fat: 26.4 g (4.1 g saturated)
Cholesterol: 78 mg
Potassium: 974 mg
Calcium: 59 mg
Sodium: 851 mg (or 131 mg if salt to taste)
Iron: 4 mg

Pretty Pomegranate Salmon p. 100
Calories: 205 kcal
Carbs: 9 g (3 g sugar, 2 g fiber)
Protein: 15 g
Fat: 13.2 g (1.9 g saturated)
Cholesterol: 24 mg
Potassium: 351 mg
Calcium: 38 mg
Sodium: 49 mg
Iron: 1 mg

"Smashed" Salmon p. 102
Calories: 216 kcal
Carbs: 0 g (0 g sugar, 0 g fiber)
Protein: 35 g
Fat: 8 g (1 g saturated)
Cholesterol: 78 mg
Potassium: 623 mg
Calcium: 12 mg
Sodium: 128 mg
Iron: <1 mg

Black Sesame-Crusted Fish p. 104
Calories: 520 kcal
Carbs: 43 g (2 g sugar, 3 g fiber)
Protein: 39 g
Fat: 20.8 g (3.8 g saturated)
Cholesterol: 94 mg
Potassium: 592 mg
Calcium: 68 mg
Sodium: 896 mg
Iron: 2 mg

Salmon with Sesame Spice Rub p. 106
Calories: 361 kcal
Carbs: 18 g (13 g sugar, 3 g fiber)
Protein: 37 g
Fat: 16.2 g (2.6 g saturated)
Cholesterol: 78 mg
Potassium: 777 mg
Calcium: 126 mg
Sodium: 1093 mg
Iron: 4 mg

Salmon with Herb Spice Rub p. 106
Calories: 313 kcal
Carbs: 17 g (13 g sugar, 1 g fiber)
Protein: 36 g
Fat: 11.1 g (1.9 g saturated)
Cholesterol: 78 mg
Potassium: 698 mg
Calcium: 39 mg
Sodium: 1093 mg
Iron: 1 mg

Salmon with Garlic Spice Rub p. 106
Calories: 300 kcal
Carbs: 14 g (11 g sugar, 1 g fiber)
Protein: 36 g
Fat: 11.2 g (1.9 g saturated)
Cholesterol: 78 mg
Potassium: 695 mg
Calcium: 25 mg
Sodium: 611 mg
Iron: 1 mg

No-Mayo Avocado Tuna Salad p. 108
Calories: 294 kcal
Carbs: 8 g (1 g sugar, 5 g fiber)
Protein: 22 g
Fat: 20.1 g (3.1 g saturated)
Cholesterol: 36 mg
Potassium: 624 mg
Calcium: 33 mg
Sodium: 529 mg
Iron: 1 mg

Crispy "Popcorn" Fish Bites p. 110
Calories: 476 kcal
Carbs: 56 g (10 g sugar, 2 g fiber)
Protein: 37 g
Fat: 10.9 g (2.0 g saturated)
Cholesterol: 149 mg
Potassium: 654 mg
Calcium: 68 mg
Sodium: 750 mg
Iron: mg

Lemon Dill Fish p. 112
Calories: 357 kcal
Carbs: 1 g (0 g sugar, 0 g fiber)
Protein: 42 g

Fat: 19.8 g (3.0 g saturated)
Cholesterol: 131 mg
Potassium: 710 mg
Calcium: 63 mg
Sodium: 591 mg
Iron: <1 mg

Seared Sriracha Honey Salmon p. 114
Calories: 358 kcal
Carbs: 15 g (12 g sugar, 1 g fiber)
Protein: 36 g
Fat: 16.6 g (2.7 g saturated)
Cholesterol: 78 mg
Potassium: 671 mg
Calcium: 60 mg
Sodium: 1209 mg (or 730 mg if salt to taste)
Iron: 2 mg

CHICKEN

Sweet Granola Chicken p. 118
Calories: 362 kcal
Carbs: 28 g (12 g sugar, 3 g fiber)
Protein: 30 g
Fat: 14.1 g (2.1 g saturated)
Cholesterol: 86 mg
Potassium: 504 mg
Calcium: 40 mg
Sodium: 65 mg
Iron: 1 mg

Sheet Pan Chicken With Heirloom Carrots and Sweet Potatoes p. 120
Calories: 406 kcal
Carbs: 24 g (15 g sugar, 3 g fiber)
Protein: 50 g
Fat: 12.0 g (2.5 g saturated)
Cholesterol: 159 mg
Potassium: 826 mg
Calcium: 59 mg
Sodium: 704 mg (or 224 mg if salt to taste)
Iron: 3 mg

Kale Chicken p. 122
Calories: 622 kcal
Carbs: 15 g (3 g sugar, 5 g fiber)

Protein: 79 g
Fat: 27.9 g (5.1 g saturated)
Cholesterol: 238 mg
Potassium: 1454 mg
Calcium: 275 mg
Sodium: 312 mg
Iron: 6 mg

Old-Fashioned BBQ Chicken p. 124
Calories: 357 kcal
Carbs: 23 g (16 g sugar, 1 g fiber)
Protein: 36 g
Fat: 13.0 g (2.3 g saturated)
Cholesterol: 115 mg
Potassium: 466 mg
Calcium: 44 mg
Sodium: 1160 mg
Iron: 2 mg

Lemon Rosemary Chicken p. 126
Calories: 250 kcal
Carbs: 3 g (1 g sugar, 1 g fiber)
Protein: 30 g
Fat: 13.2 g (2.7 g saturated)
Cholesterol: 140 mg
Potassium: 397 mg
Calcium: 24 mg
Sodium: 782 mg
Iron: 1 mg

Salami Hasselback Chicken p. 128
Calories: 481 kcal
Carbs: 27 g (20 g sugar, 0 g fiber)
Protein: 57 g
Fat: 14.6 g (5.0 g saturated)
Cholesterol: 179 mg
Potassium: 1198 mg
Calcium: 18 mg
Sodium: 1810 mg
Iron: 3 mg

Rustic Sheet Pan Chicken p. 130
Calories: 801 kcal
Carbs: 71 g (35 g sugar, 13 g fiber)
Protein: 84 g
Fat: 19.5 g (3.8 g saturated)
Cholesterol: 238 mg
Potassium: 1697 mg
Calcium: 183 mg
Sodium: 860 mg
Iron: 7 mg

Glazed Grilled Chicken p. 132
Calories: 212 kcal
Carbs: 7 g (6 g sugar, 1 g fiber)
Protein: 27 g
Fat: 8.0 g (1 g saturated)
Cholesterol: 86 mg
Potassium: 442 mg
Calcium: 18 mg
Sodium: 456 mg
Iron: 1 mg

Tomato Garlic Chicken p. 134
Calories: 314 kcal
Carbs: 14 g (11 g sugar, 1 g fiber)
Protein: 36 g
Fat: 12.3 g (2.3 g saturated)
Cholesterol: 114 mg
Potassium: 612 mg
Calcium: 46 mg
Sodium: 613 mg
Iron: 2 mg

Baked Almond Flour Chicken p. 136
Calories: 509 kcal
Carbs: 10 g (2 g sugar, 5 g fiber)
Protein: 55 g
Fat: 29.0 g (4.1 g saturated)
Cholesterol: 264 mg
Potassium: 573 mg
Calcium: 114 mg
Sodium: 775 mg
Iron: 4 mg

Honey Glazed Sunflower Seed Chicken p. 138
Calories: 353 kcal
Carbs: 14 g (9 g sugar, 3 g fiber)
Protein: 31 g
Fat: 20.5 g (2.7 g saturated)
Cholesterol: 86 mg
Potassium: 528 mg
Calcium: 24 mg
Sodium: 56 mg
Iron: 2 mg

Spaghetti Squash Chicken p. 140
Calories: 539 kcal
Carbs: 28 g (13 g sugar, 6 g fiber)
Protein: 76 g
Fat: 12.7 g (3.1 g saturated)

Cholesterol: 240 mg
Potassium: 1457 mg
Calcium: 143 mg
Sodium: 684 mg
Iron: 5 mg

Potato Latke Schnitzel p. 142
Calories: 340 kcal
Carbs: 44 g (3 g sugar, 4 g fiber)
Protein: 33 g
Fat: 4.7 g (1.2 g saturated)
Cholesterol: 148 mg
Potassium: 539 mg
Calcium: 201 mg
Sodium: 461 mg
Iron: 3 mg

Honey Mustard Chicken and Steak Dinner p. 144
Calories: 525 kcal
Carbs: 17 g (16 g sugar, 0 g fiber)
Protein: 60 g
Fat: 21.9 g (6.7 g saturated)
Cholesterol: 186 mg
Potassium: 785 mg
Calcium: 35 mg
Sodium: 1285 mg
Iron: 5 mg

MEAT

Skirt Steak Strips With Tahini Herb Sauce p. 148
Calories: 639 kcal
Carbs: 13 g (8 g sugar, 1 g fiber)
Protein: 64 g
Fat: 35.9 g (10.6 g saturated)
Cholesterol: 193 mg
Potassium: 795 mg
Calcium: 64 mg
Sodium: 784 mg
Iron: 8 mg

Sesame-Crusted London Broil p. 150
Calories: 420 kcal
Carbs: 11 g (9 g sugar, 1 g fiber)
Protein: 56 g
Fat: 15.7 g (4.0 g saturated)
Cholesterol: 136 mg

Potassium: 532 mg
Calcium: 51 mg
Sodium: 580 mg
Iron: 6 mg

Bruschetta London Broil p. 152
Calories: 383 kcal
Carbs: 7 g (3 g sugar, 1 g fiber)
Protein: 56 g
Fat: 13.7 g (3.7 g saturated)
Cholesterol: 136 mg
Potassium: 758 mg
Calcium: 26 mg
Sodium: 394 mg
Iron: 6 mg

Marinated Hot Pepper Brisket p. 154
Calories: 737 kcal
Carbs: 16 g (12 g sugar, 2 g fiber)
Protein: 63 g
Fat: 45.3 g (17.2 g saturated)
Cholesterol: 212 mg
Potassium: 874 mg
Calcium: 44 mg
Sodium: 1020 mg (636 mg without 2 tsp kosher salt)
Iron: 7 mg

Saucy Miami Ribs With Parsnips p. 156
Calories: 178 kcal
Carbs: 25 g (13 g sugar, 4 g fiber)
Protein: 10 g
Fat: 4.5 g (1.7 g saturated)
Cholesterol: 23 mg
Potassium: 544 mg
Calcium: 58 mg
Sodium: 639 mg
Iron: 2 mg

Brisket Ends p. 158
Calories: 295 kcal
Carbs: 22 g (18 g sugar, 1 g fiber)
Protein: 24 g
Fat: 12.2 g (3.5 g saturated)
Cholesterol: 70 mg
Potassium: 490 mg
Calcium: 25 mg
Sodium: 1022 mg (or 441 mg if salt to taste)
Iron: 3 mg

Smothered Short Ribs p. 160
Calories: 830 kcal
Carbs: 12 g (10 g sugar, 1 g fiber)
Protein: 87 g
Fat: 46.3 g (19.7 g saturated)
Cholesterol: 268 mg
Potassium: 1747 mg
Calcium: 46 mg
Sodium: 329 mg
Iron: 10 mg

Meatballs With Mushrooms p. 162
Calories: 354 kcal
Carbs: 23 g (16 g sugar, 1 g fiber)
Protein: 33 g
Fat: 15.4 g (6.0 g saturated)
Cholesterol: 98 mg
Potassium: 931 mg
Calcium: 44 mg
Sodium: 1062 mg
Iron: 4 mg

Overnight Shabbos Corned Beef p. 164
Calories: 429 kcal
Carbs: 6 g (3 g sugar, 1 g fiber)
Protein: 25 g
Fat: 35.4 g (12.8 g saturated)
Cholesterol: 121 mg
Potassium: 54 mg
Calcium: 16 mg
Sodium: 3 mg
Iron: 3 mg

Taco Bowl Night p. 166
(analysis includes suggested toppings)
Calories: 404 kcal
Carbs: 38 g (3 g sugar, 3 g fiber)
Protein: 28 g
Fat: 16.5 g (4.8 g saturated)
Cholesterol: 74 mg
Potassium: 531 mg
Calcium: 26 mg
Sodium: 591 mg (or 111 mg if salt to taste)
Iron: 4 mg

DAIRY

Pull-Apart Eggplant Parmesan p. 170
Calories: 282 kcal
Carbs: 20 g (11 g sugar, 6 g fiber)
Protein: 19 g
Fat: 14.9 g (7.7 g saturated)
Cholesterol: 44 mg
Potassium: 788 mg
Calcium: 506 mg
Sodium: 876 mg
Iron: 2 mg

Low-Cal Cauliflower Mushroom Risotto p. 172
Calories: 126 kcal
Carbs: 10 g (4 g sugar, 3 g fiber)
Protein: 7 g
Fat: 7.4 g (2.8 g saturated)
Cholesterol: 13 mg
Potassium: 536 mg
Calcium: 189 mg
Sodium: 929 mg (or 209 mg if salt to taste)
Iron: <1 mg

Summery Feta Salad p. 174
Calories: 190 kcal
Carbs: 10 g (6 g sugar, 3 g fiber)
Protein: 4 g
Fat: 15.8 g (4.4 g saturated)
Cholesterol: 17 mg
Potassium: 227 mg
Calcium: 126 mg
Sodium: 475 mg
Iron: 1 mg

Zoodle Cheese Nests p. 176
Calories: 35 kcal
Carbs: 3 g (2 g sugar, 0.7 g fiber)
Protein: 4 g
Fat: 1.2 g (0.6 g saturated)
Cholesterol: 3 mg
Potassium: 183 mg
Calcium: 59 mg
Sodium: 160 mg
Iron: <1 mg

Crustless Baby Red Potato Quiche p. 178

Calories: 431 kcal (324 kcal)

Carbs: 70 g (7 g sugar, 7 g fiber)
(52 g (5 g sugar, 5 g fiber)

Protein: 21 g (16 g protein)

Fat: 7.1 g (3.4 g saturated)
(5.3 g (2.5 g saturated)

Cholesterol: 135 mg (101 mg)

Potassium: 2024 mg (1518 mg)

Calcium: 204 mg (153 mg)

Sodium: 1004 mg (753 mg)

Iron: 4 mg (3 mg)

Cheesy Seed Crisps p. 180

Calories: 94 kcal

Carbs: 5 g (0 g sugar, 1 g fiber)

Protein: 6 g

Fat: 5.9 g (1.3 g saturated)

Cholesterol: 3 mg

Potassium: 81 mg

Calcium: 81 mg

Sodium: 261 mg

Iron: <1 mg

Keto Cheese Crust Pizza p. 182

Calories: 237 kcal

Carbs: 13 g (6 g sugar, 2 g fiber)

Protein: 17 g

Fat: 13.2 g (6.8 g saturated)

Cholesterol: 140 mg

Potassium: 298 mg

Calcium: 402 mg

Sodium: 448 mg

Iron: 1 mg

Granola Crusted "Breakfast" Tart p. 184

Calories: 295 kcal

Carbs: 35 g (18 g sugar, 5 g fiber)

Protein: 13 g

Fat: 13.1 g (2.6 g saturated)

Cholesterol: 4 mg

Potassium: 317 mg

Calcium: 119 mg

Sodium: 38 mg

Iron: 1 mg

Baked Broccoli Tots p. 186

Calories: 39 kcal

Carbs: 4 g (1 g sugar, 1 g fiber)

Protein: 3 g

Fat: 1.4 g (0.6 g saturated)

Cholesterol: 26 mg

Potassium: 67 mg

Calcium: 37 mg

Sodium: 161 mg

Iron: 0 mg

5-Ingredient Cauliflower Cheese Bites p. 188

(4 per serving)

Calories: 62 kcal

Carbs: 3 g (1 g sugar, 1 g fiber)

Protein: 11 g

Fat: 0.9 g (0.3 g saturated)

Cholesterol: 36 mg

Potassium: 153 mg

Calcium: 286 mg

Sodium: 233 mg

Iron: 0.4 mg

Avocado Pesto Spaghetti p. 190

Calories: 524 kcal

Carbs: 67 g (4 g sugar, 9 g fiber)

Protein: 19 g

Fat: 21.5 g (3.2 g saturated)

Cholesterol: 4 mg

Potassium: 765 mg

Calcium: 122 mg

Sodium: 418 mg

Iron: 5 mg

Lazy Hash and Egg Dinner p. 192

Calories: 327 kcal

Carbs: 24 g (10 g sugar, 4 g fiber)

Protein: 14 g

Fat: 20.1 g (8.2 g saturated)

Cholesterol: 219 mg

Potassium: 596 mg

Calcium: 265 mg

Sodium: 1294 mg

Iron: 2 mg

GRAIN SIDES

Crispy Garlic Couscous p. 196

Calories: 302 kcal

Carbs: 55 g (4 g sugar, 4 g fiber)

Protein: 9 g

Fat: 5.2 g (0.8 g saturated)

Cholesterol: 0 mg

Potassium: 307 mg

Calcium: 32 mg

Sodium: 683 mg

Iron: <1 mg

Jasmine Coconut and Cranberry Rice p. 198

Calories: 398 kcal

Carbs: 50 g (9 g sugar, 5 g fiber)

Protein: 8 g

Fat: 21.1 g (10.1 g saturated)

Cholesterol: 0 mg

Potassium: 124 mg

Calcium: 47 mg

Sodium: 328 mg

Iron: 2 mg

Candied Brown Rice Salad p. 200

Calories: 361 kcal

Carbs: 34 g (4 g sugar, 5 g fiber)

Protein: 10 g

Fat: 22.2 g (2.6 g saturated)

Cholesterol: 0 mg

Potassium: 335 mg

Calcium: 58 mg

Sodium: 6 mg

Iron: 2 mg

Mediterranean Quinoa Salad p. 202

Calories: 580 kcal

Carbs: 66 g (6 g sugar, 14 g fiber)

Protein: 19 g

Fat: 28.7 g (3.6 g saturated)

Cholesterol: 0 mg

Potassium: 968 mg

Calcium: 178 mg

Sodium: 522 mg

Iron: 6 mg

Spicy Roasted Cauliflower and Chickpea Salad p. 204

Calories: 266 kcal

Carbs: 30 g (4 g sugar, 11 g fiber)

Protein: 10 g

Fat: 14.3 g (2.5 g saturated)

Cholesterol: 0 mg

Potassium: 657 mg

Calcium: 90 mg

Sodium: 482 mg

Iron: 3 mg

Asian Rice Salad With Wasabi Peas p. 206

Calories: 444 kcal

Carbs: 48 g (14 g sugar, 5 g fiber)

Protein: 10 g

Fat: 26.2 g (4.2 g saturated)

Cholesterol: 0 mg

Potassium: 466 mg

Calcium: 75 mg

Sodium: 1257 mg (or 937 mg if salt to taste)

Iron: 2 mg

Roasted Onion Quinoa Salad p. 208

Calories: 289 kcal

Carbs: 25 g (3 g sugar, 6 g fiber)

Protein: 5 g

Fat: 20.2 g (2.9 g saturated)

Cholesterol: 0 mg

Potassium: 435 mg

Calcium: 38 mg

Sodium: 406 mg

Iron: 2 mg

Fresh Orzo Salad p. 210

Calories: 384 kcal

Carbs: 51 g (4 g sugar, 6 g fiber)

Protein: 12 g

Fat: 15.2 g (2.1 g saturated)

Cholesterol: 0 mg

Potassium: 302 mg

Calcium: 65 mg

Sodium: 403 mg

Iron: 3 mg

Crouton Farro Salad p. 212

Calories: 243 kcal

Carbs: 29 g (6 g sugar, 3 g fiber)

Protein: 5 g

Fat: 13.1 g (1.9 g saturated)

Cholesterol: 0 mg

Potassium: 121 mg

Calcium: 49 mg

Sodium: 74 mg

Iron: <1 mg

VEGETABLE SIDES

Garlic Shishito Peppers p. 216

Calories: 54 kcal

Carbs: 5 g (3 g sugar, 1 g fiber)

Protein: 1 g

Fat: 3.8 g (0.5 g saturated)

Cholesterol: 0 mg

Potassium: 187 mg

Calcium: 8 mg

Sodium: 5 mg

Iron: <1 mg

Maple-Glazed Japanese Sweet Potatoes p. 218

Calories: 175 kcal

Carbs: 28 g (10 g sugar, 4 g fiber)

Protein: 2 g

Fat: 7.1 g (1.0 g saturated)

Cholesterol: 0 mg

Potassium: 358 mg

Calcium: 56 mg

Sodium: 535 mg

Iron: <1 mg

Lemon-Mint Mini Peppers p. 220

Calories: 140 kcal

Carbs: 24 g (18 g sugar, 5 g fiber)

Protein: 3 g

Fat: 4.3 g (0.6 g saturated)

Cholesterol: 0 mg

Potassium: 535 mg

Calcium: 35 mg

Sodium: 252 mg

Iron: 2 mg

"Everything Bagel" Asparagus p. 222

Calories: 102 kcal

Carbs: 9 g (3 g sugar, 4 g fiber)

Protein: 5 g

Fat: 6.9 g (1.0 g saturated)

Cholesterol: 0 mg

Potassium: 362 mg

Calcium: 90 mg

Sodium: 391 mg

Iron: 4 mg

Spiced Eggplant Wedges p. 224

Calories: 114 kcal

Carbs: 13 g (8 g sugar, 4 g fiber)

Protein: 2 g

Fat: 7.3 g (1.1 g saturated)

Cholesterol: 0 mg

Potassium: 349 mg

Calcium: 20 mg

Sodium: 628 mg

Iron: <1 mg

Pretty Roasted Onion Flowers p. 226

Calories: 150 kcal

Carbs: 7 g (3 g sugar, 2 g fiber)

Protein: 1 g

Fat: 13.6 g (1.9 g saturated)

Cholesterol: 0 mg

Potassium: 111 mg

Calcium: 35 mg

Sodium: 4 mg

Iron: 2 mg

Chip-Topped Green Beans p. 228

Calories: 202 kcal

Carbs: 27 g (6 g sugar, 6 g fiber)

Protein: 6 g

Fat: 9.8 g (1.4 g saturated)

Cholesterol: 0 mg

Potassium: 793 mg

Calcium: 68 mg

Sodium: 530 mg

Iron: 3 mg

Herbed Honey-Roasted Tomatoes p. 230

Calories: 126 kcal

Carbs: 11 g (9 g sugar, 1 g fiber)

Protein: 1 g

Fat: 9.6 g (1.4 g saturated)

Cholesterol: 0 mg

Potassium: 251 mg

Calcium: 21 mg

Sodium: 326 mg

Iron: <1 mg

Dilled Roasted Cauliflower and Broccoli p. 232

Calories: 132 kcal

Carbs: 16 g (9 g sugar, 4 g fiber)

Protein: 4 g

Fat: 7.5 g (1.2 g saturated)

Cholesterol: 0 mg

Potassium: 551 mg

Calcium: 53 mg

Sodium: 376 mg

Iron: <1 mg

Peanut Butter Sweet Potatoes p. 234

Calories: 429 kcal

Carbs: 31 g (13 g sugar, 6 g fiber)

Protein: 12 g

Fat: 27 g (4.1 g saturated)

Cholesterol: 0 mg

Potassium: 225 mg

Calcium: 26 mg

Sodium: 144 mg

Iron: 1 mg

Steamed Broccoli With Ginger Topping p. 236

Calories: 63 kcal

Carbs: 4 g (1 g sugar, 1 g fiber)

Protein: 2 g

Fat: 4.9 g (0.7 g saturated)

Cholesterol: 0 mg

Potassium: 166 mg

Calcium: 28 mg

Sodium: 300 mg

Iron: <1 mg

Salted Baby Potatoes p. 238

Calories: 165 kcal

Carbs: 24 g (2 g sugar, 3 g fiber)

Protein: 3 g

Fat: 7 g (1 g saturated)

Cholesterol: 0 mg

Potassium: 683 mg

Calcium: 15 mg

Sodium: 6915 mg (It was assumed that only 15% of sodium used was absorbed into potatoes after excess salt was discarded)

Iron: 1 mg

Hash Brown "Potato Kugel" Waffles p. 240

Calories: 321 kcal

Carbs: 58 g (4 g sugar, 6 g fiber)

Protein: 7 g

Fat: 10.1 g (1.6 g saturated)

Cholesterol: 35 mg

Potassium: 47 mg

Calcium: 230 mg

Sodium: 1069 mg

Iron: 3 mg

DESSERT

Double Chocolate Banana Cake p. 244

Calories: 410 kcal

Carbs: 57 g (33 g sugar, 4 g fiber)

Protein: 6 g

Fat: 20.3 g (6.0 g saturated)

Cholesterol: 37 mg

Potassium: 370 mg

Calcium: 57 mg

Sodium: 149 mg

Iron: 3 mg

Chocolate Covered Chickpeas p. 246

Calories: 274 kcal

Carbs: 38 g (23 g sugar, 6 g fiber)

Protein: 6 g

Fat: 14.3 g (7.7 g saturated)

Cholesterol: 0 mg

Potassium: 270 mg

Calcium: 42 mg

Sodium: 227 mg

Iron: 2 mg

Strawberry Almond Tart p. 248

Calories: 390 kcal

Carbs: 32 g (20 g sugar, 5 g fiber)

Protein: 7 g

Fat: 27.8 g (2.1 g saturated)

Cholesterol: 0 mg

Potassium: 217 mg

Calcium: 54 mg

Sodium: 304 mg

Iron: 2 mg

Peanut Butter Chocolate Popcorn p. 250

Calories: 236 kcal

Carbs: 29 g (17 g sugar, 3 g fiber)

Protein: 5 g

Fat: 13.6 g (5.9 g saturated)

Cholesterol: 0 mg

Potassium: 123 mg

Calcium: 18 mg

Sodium: 83 mg

Iron: 1 mg

Low-Fat Ginger Biscotti p. 252

Calories: 168 kcal

Carbs: 21 g (11 g sugar, 2 g fiber)

Protein: 3 g

Fat: 8.7 g (2.6 g saturated)

Cholesterol: 18 mg

Potassium: 111 mg

Calcium: 38 mg

Sodium: 70 mg

Iron: <1 mg

Mint Chocolate Chip Cookies p. 254

Calories: 375 kcal

Carbs: 52 g (32 g sugar, 2 g fiber)

Protein: 4 g

Fat: 18.4 g (5.1 g saturated)

Cholesterol: 25 mg

Potassium: 138 mg

Calcium: 16 mg

Sodium: 98 mg

Iron: 2 mg

Espresso Chocolate Chip Cookies p. 256

Calories: 352 kcal

Carbs: 40 g (21 g sugar, 1 g fiber)

Protein: 3 g

Fat: 20.0 g (3.2 g saturated)

Cholesterol: 26 mg

Potassium: 125 mg

Calcium: 30 mg

Sodium: 171 mg

Iron: 2 mg

Black and White Moist Chocolate Cake p. 258

Calories: 519 kcal

Carbs: 86 g (60 g sugar, 5 g fiber)

Protein: 7 g

Fat: 19.0 g (5.5 g saturated)

Cholesterol: 39 mg

Potassium: 344 mg

Calcium: 82 mg

Sodium: 154 mg

Iron: 4 mg

Classic Fruit Flan p. 260

Calories: 496 kcal
Carbs: 43 g (22 g sugar, 2 g fiber)
Protein: 7 g
Fat: 34.0 g (3.3 g saturated)
Cholesterol: 116 mg
Potassium: 171 mg
Calcium: 32 mg
Sodium: 47 mg
Iron: 2 mg

The Blue Cake p. 262

Calories: 467 kcal
Carbs: 60 g (39 g sugar, 1 g fiber)
Protein: 4 g
Fat: 24.1 g (2.1 g saturated)
Cholesterol: 47 mg
Potassium: 145 mg
Calcium: 30 mg
Sodium: 178 mg
Iron: 2 mg

Coconut Chocolate Tart p. 264

Calories: 562 kcal
Carbs: 31 g (24 g sugar, 4 g fiber)
Protein: 6 g
Fat: 48.5 g (32.7 g saturated)
Cholesterol: 80 mg
Potassium: 175 mg
Calcium: 97mg
Sodium: 63 mg
Iron: 1 mg

Coconut Strawberry Shortcake p. 266

Calories: 594 kcal
Carbs: 61 g (34 g sugar, 3 g fiber)

Protein: 6 g
Fat: 37.1 g (7.5 g saturated)
Cholesterol: 84 mg
Potassium: 338 mg
Calcium: 67 mg
Sodium: 223 mg
Iron: 2 mg

Olive Oil Salted Brownies p. 268

Calories: 329 kcal
Carbs: 45 g (37 g sugar, 3 g fiber)
Protein: 4 g
Fat: 17.9 g (7.1 g saturated)
Cholesterol: 47 mg
Potassium: 230 mg
Calcium: 49 mg
Sodium: 22 mg
Iron: 2 mg

Rose Petal Apple Tart p. 270

Calories: 281 kcal
Carbs: 33 g (15 g sugar, 3 g fiber)
Protein: 2 g
Fat: 16.5 g (1.2 g saturated)
Cholesterol: 0 mg
Potassium: 94 mg
Calcium: 11 mg
Sodium: 1 mg
Iron: 1 mg

Afternoon Snack Bars p. 272

Calories: 255 kcal
Carbs: 34 g (22 g sugar, 4 g fiber)
Protein: 6 g
Fat: 12.2 g (3.2 g saturated)
Cholesterol: 1 mg
Potassium: 203 mg
Calcium: 27 mg

Sodium: 44 mg
Iron: 1 mg

Cayenne-Lime Mango and Watermelon p. 274

Calories: 232 kcal
Carbs: 61 g (51 g sugar, 6 g fiber)
Protein: 3 g
Fat: 0.8 g (0.2 g saturated)
Cholesterol: 0 mg
Potassium: 726 mg
Calcium: 68 mg
Sodium: 3 mg
Iron: 2 mg

Dragon Fruit Salad p. 276

Calories: 81 kcal
Carbs: 21 g (14 4 sugar, g fiber)
Protein: 1 g
Fat: 0.5 g (0 g saturated)
Cholesterol: 0 mg
Potassium: 192 mg
Calcium: 21 mg
Sodium: 2 mg
Iron: <1 mg

Candied Marshmallow Lollipops p. 278

Calories: 303 kcal
Carbs: 55 g (41 g sugar, 2 g fiber)
Protein: 2 g
Fat: 11.3 g (4.6 g saturated)
Cholesterol: 0 mg
Potassium: 95 mg
Calcium: 9 mg
Sodium: 30 mg
Iron: 1 mg

INDEX

A

ALMONDS
BBQ Romaine Salad, 77
Candied Brown Rice Salad, 200
Crunch Topping, 201
Endive Boat Salad, 67
Fresh Herb Granola Salad, 66
Granola Crusted "Breakfast" Tart, 184
High-Fiber Salad Topper, 88
Jasmine Coconut and Cranberry Rice, 198
Kale Rice Rolls, 71
Mediterranean Quinoa Salad, 202
Panko-Topped Kale Salad, 70
Peach Crisps, 249
Rainbow Bright Salad, 80
Shredded Kale and Brussels Sprouts Salad, 74
Strawberry Almond Tart, 248
Sweet Granola Chicken, 118
Three-Toned Cabbage Salad, 84

APPLES
Apple Crisps, 271
Rose Petal Apple Tart, 270

ARUGULA
Baked Mini Falafel Ball Salad, 82
Candied Brown Rice Salad, 200

ASPARAGUS
Asparagus and Rice, 223
Bread Cup Ideas, 33
"Everything Bagel" Asparagus, 222
Lemon Herbed Salmon Rolls with Asparagus, 98

AVOCADOS
Avocado Lentil Salad, 68
Avocado Pesto Spaghetti, 190
Baked Mini Falafel Ball Salad, 82
Black and White Avocado Salad, 72
Brisket Boats, 159
Crunchy Chicken Kale Salad, 22
Deli Egg Rolls, 24
Deli Rice Rolls, 25
Hawaiian Poke Bowl, 92
Kale Falafel, 83
Lentil Cauliflower Salad, 205
Mediterranean Quinoa Salad, 202
No-Mayo Avocado Tuna Salad, 108
Roasted Onion Quinoa Salad, 208
Roasted Pepper Wraps, 221
Spicy Roasted Cauliflower and Chickpea Salad, 204
Summery Feta Salad, 174
Topped Sriracha Salmon, 115
Tuna Nachos, 109
Zaatar Avocado, 30

B

Bagels, Salmon, 97

BANANAS
Double Chocolate Banana Cake, 244
Double Chocolate Muffins, 245

Barley Poke Bowl, 213

BASIL
Avocado Pesto Spaghetti, 190
Bruschetta London Broil, 152
Fresh Orzo Salad, 210
London Broil Crostini, 153
Orzo Pepper Cups, 211
Skirt Steak Strips with Tahini Herb Sauce, 148

BEANS. SEE ALSO CHICKPEAS; GREEN BEANS
Avocado Pesto Spaghetti, 190
Candied Brown Rice Salad, 200
Dinner Steak Soup, 58

BEEF
Bone Marrow Spread, 35
Brisket Boats, 159
Brisket Ends, 158
Bruschetta London Broil, 152
Club Sandwiches, 165
Corned Beef Biscotti, 26
Corned Beef Topped Eggplant, 14
Deli Egg Rolls, 24
Deli Hash Brown Pizza, 241
Deli Rice Rolls, 25
Deli-Wrapped Squash Bites, 20
Dinner Steak Soup, 58
Honey Mustard Chicken and Steak Dinner, 144
Lemon Herbed Bone Marrow, 34
London Broil Crostini, 153
Marinated Hot Pepper Brisket, 154
Meatball Mushroom Sloppy Joes, 163
Meatballs with Mushrooms, 162
Overnight Shabbos Corned Beef, 164
Rice Noodle Dinner, 145
Salami Hasselback Chicken, 128
Saucy Miami Ribs with Parsnips, 156
Sesame-Crusted London Broil, 150
Short Rib Chunks with Rice, 161
Skirt Steak Strips with Tahini Herb Sauce, 148
Skirt Steak Tahini Salad, 149
Smothered Short Ribs, 160
Sweet Potato Brisket, 155
Taco Bowl Night, 166

BEETS
Feta Quinoa Hash, 193
Lazy Hash and Egg Dinner, 192
Zoodle Cheese Nests, 176
Zoodle Lasagna, 177

BERRIES. SEE ALSO SPECIFIC BERRIES
Berry Cups, 267
Ginger Berry Cups, 253
Granola Crusted "Breakfast" Tart, 184

BISCOTTI
Corned Beef Biscotti, 26
Low-Fat Ginger Biscotti, 252

BLUEBERRIES
Dragon Fruit Salad, 276
Rainbow Bright Salad, 80
Summery Feta Salad, 174

BONE MARROW
Bone Marrow Spread, 35
Lemon Herbed Bone Marrow, 34

BREAD-BASED RECIPES. SEE ALSO SANDWICHES
Bread Cup Ideas, 33
Cute Baguette Cups, 32
London Broil Crostini, 153
Soup Bread Bowls, 57

BREAD CRUMBS. SEE PANKO

BROCCOLI
Baked Broccoli Tots, 186
Broccoli Tart, 187

Caramelized Leek and Broccoli Soup, 54
Cute Baguette Cups, 32
Dilled Roasted Cauliflower and Broccoli, 232
Steamed Broccoli with Ginger Topping, 236
Brownies, Olive Oil Salted, 268
Bruschetta London Broil, 152

BRUSSELS SPROUTS
Pretty Brussels Sprouts Salad, 78
Quinoa Brussels Sprouts Salad, 79
Shredded Kale and Brussels Sprouts Salad, 74

C

CABBAGE
Asian Rice Salad with Wasabi Peas, 206
Barley Poke Bowl, 213
Crouton Farro Salad, 212
Gingery Steamed Cabbage, 237
Rainbow Bright Salad, 80
Summery Feta Salad, 174
Three-Toned Cabbage Salad, 84
Caesar Crisp Salad, 181

CAKES
Black and White Moist Chocolate Cake, 258
Blue Cake, The, 262
Double Chocolate Banana Cake, 244
Marshmallow Cake, 279
Salted Brownie Cake, 269

CARROTS
Cute Baguette Cups, 32
Healthy Tomato Lentil Soup, 50
Rainbow Bright Salad, 80
Rustic Couscous, 131
Rustic Sheet Pan Chicken, 130
Sheet Pan Chicken with Heirloom Carrots and Sweet Potatoes, 120
Spiralized Noodle Soup, 48
Vegetarian Vegetable Quinoa Soup, 52
Zoodle Cheese Nests, 176
Zoodle Chicken Soup, 49
Zoodle Lasagna, 177

CASHEWS
Fresh Orzo Salad, 210
Orzo Pepper Cups, 211
Pretty Brussels Sprouts Salad, 78
Quinoa Brussels Sprouts Salad, 79
Rainbow Bright Salad, 80

CAULIFLOWER
Caramelized Leek and Cauliflower Soup, 55
Cauliflower Quiche, 189
Dilled Roasted Cauliflower and Broccoli, 232
5-Ingredient Cauliflower Cheese Bites, 188
Lentil Cauliflower Salad, 205
Low Cal Cauliflower Mushroom Risotto, 172
Spicy Roasted Cauliflower and Chickpea Salad, 204

CELERY
Endive Boat Salad, 67
Fresh Herb Granola Salad, 66
Healing Celery Soup, 40
Pretty Brussels Sprouts Salad, 78
Quinoa Brussels Sprouts Salad, 79

CHEESE
Baked Broccoli Tots, 186
Broccoli Tart, 187
Cauliflower Quiche, 189
Cheesy Seed Crisps, 180
Crustless Baby Red Potato Quiche, 178
Cucumber Roll Ups, 28
Feta Quinoa Hash, 193
5-Ingredient Cauliflower Cheese Bites, 188
Keto Cheese Crust Pizza, 182
Lazy Hash and Egg Dinner, 192
Low Cal Cauliflower Mushroom Risotto, 172
Pull-Apart Eggplant Parmesan, 170
Salmon Bagels, 97
Summery Feta Salad, 174
Zoodle Cheese Nests, 176
Zoodle Lasagna, 177

CHICKEN
Baked Almond Flour Chicken, 136
Crunchy Chicken Kale Salad, 22
Dill Pickle Football Wings, 36
Glazed Grilled Chicken, 132
Grilled Chicken Skewers, 133
Honey-Glazed Sunflower Seed Chicken, 138
Honey Mustard Chicken and Steak Dinner, 144
Kale Chicken, 122
Lemon Rosemary Chicken, 126
Old-Fashioned BBQ Chicken, 124
Potato Latke Schnitzel, 142
Pumpkin Seed Chicken, 139
Rice Noodle Dinner, 145
Rustic Sheet Pan Chicken, 130
Salami Hasselback Chicken, 128
Sheet Pan Chicken with Heirloom Carrots and Sweet Potatoes, 120
Spaghetti Squash Chicken, 140
Sweet Granola Chicken, 118
Sweet Potato Schnitzel, 143
Tomato Garlic Chicken, 134
Zoodle Chicken Soup, 49

CHICKPEAS
Baked Mini Falafel Ball Salad, 82

Black and White Avocado Salad, 72
Chocolate Covered Chickpeas, 246
Fresh Orzo Salad, 210
Kale Falafel, 83
Mediterranean Quinoa Salad, 202
Orzo Pepper Cups, 211
Rustic Couscous, 131
Rustic Sheet Pan Chicken, 130
Spicy Roasted Cauliflower and Chickpea Salad, 204
Tofu Soup, 59

CHOCOLATE
Afternoon Snack Bars, 272
Black and White Moist Chocolate Cake, 258
Candied Marshmallow Lollipops, 278
Chocolate Covered Chickpeas, 246
Coconut Chocolate Tart, 264
Double Chocolate Banana Cake, 244
Double Chocolate Muffins, 245
Espresso Chocolate Chip Cookies, 256
Granola Balls, 273
Ice Cream Sandwiches, 255
Marshmallow Cake, 279
Mint Chocolate Chip Cookies, 254
Olive Oil Salted Brownies, 268
Peanut Butter Chocolate Popcorn, 250
Salted Brownie Cake, 269
Cinnamon Sugar Pears, 43

COCONUT
Coconut Chocolate Tart, 264
Coconut Strawberry Shortcake, 266
Granola Crusted "Breakfast" Tart, 184
High-Fiber Salad Topper, 88
Jasmine Coconut and Cranberry Rice, 198

COOKIES
Corned Beef Biscotti, 26
Espresso Chocolate Chip Cookies, 256
Ice Cream Sandwiches, 255
Low-Fat Ginger Biscotti, 252
Mint Chocolate Chip Cookies, 254

CORN
Dinner Steak Soup, 58
Rainbow Bright Salad, 80
Tofu Soup, 59

COUSCOUS
Crispy Garlic Couscous, 196
Rustic Couscous, 131

CRANBERRIES
Afternoon Snack Bars, 272
Endive Boat Salad, 67
Fresh Herb Granola Salad, 66
Granola Balls, 273
Jasmine Coconut and Cranberry Rice, 198
Pea Shoot Salad, 64

Rainbow Bright Salad, 80
Shredded Kale and Brussels Sprouts
Salad, 74
Crostini, London Broil, 153
Crouton Farro Salad, 212
CUCUMBERS
Cucumber Roll Ups, 28
Cute Baguette Cups, 32
Fresh Orzo Salad, 210
Hawaiian Poke Bowl, 92
Hemp Heart Cucumber Salad, 86
No-Mayo Avocado Tuna Salad, 108
Orzo Pepper Cups, 211
Rainbow Bright Salad, 80
Roasted Pepper Wraps, 221
Tuna Nachos, 109

D

DILL
Dilled Roasted Cauliflower and Broccoli,
232
Lemon Dill Fish, 112
Pepper Dill Fish, 113
Dill Pickle Football Wings, 36
Dragon Fruit Salad, 276

E

EGGPLANT
Corned Beef Topped Eggplant, 14
Hummus Eggplant Topper, 225
Mediterranean Quinoa Salad, 202
Pull-Apart Eggplant Parmesan, 170
Spiced Eggplant Wedges, 224
Egg Rolls, Deli, 24
EGGS
Cucumber Roll Ups, 28
Lazy Hash and Egg Dinner, 192
Endive Boat Salad, 67
Espresso Chocolate Chip Cookies, 256
"Everything Bagel" Asparagus, 222

F

FALAFEL
Baked Mini Falafel Ball Salad, 82
Kale Falafel, 83
Farro, Crouton Salad, 212

Fig Salmon, 101
FISH. *SEE ALSO* **SALMON**
Black Sesame–Crusted Fish, 104
Crispy "Popcorn" Fish Bites, 110
Fish Tacos, 105
Hawaiian Poke Bowl, 92
Lemon Dill Fish, 112
No-Mayo Avocado Tuna Salad, 108
Pepper Dill Fish, 113
Tuna Nachos, 109
Flan, Classic Fruit, 260
FRUIT. *SEE ALSO* **SPECIFIC FRUITS**
Classic Fruit Flan, 260
Lemon Parfait, 261
Rustic Couscous, 131
Rustic Sheet Pan Chicken, 130

G

GARLIC
Crispy Garlic Coucous, 196
Garlic Shishito Peppers, 216
Gingery Steamed Cabbage, 237
Salmon with 3 Spice Rubs, 106
Steamed Broccoli wiith Ginger Topping, 236
Toasted Garlic Panko Topping, 44
Tomato Garlic Chicken, 134
GINGER
Ginger Berry Cups, 253
Gingery Steamed Cabbage, 237
Low-Fat Ginger Biscotti, 252
Steamed Broccoli wiith Ginger Topping, 236
Granola Balls, 273
Granola Crusted "Breakfast" Tart, 184
GREEN BEANS
Chip-Topped Green Beans, 228
Green Bean Salad, 229
GREENS. *SEE ALSO* **SPECIFIC GREENS**
Roasted Pepper Wraps, 221
Salad Bowls, 219

H

Hawaiian Poke Bowl, 92
HEMP HEARTS
Hemp Heart Cucumber Salad, 86
High-Fiber Salad Topper, 88
HERBS. *SEE ALSO* **BASIL; DILL; MINT;
PARSLEY**
Endive Boat Salad, 67

Fresh Herb Granola Salad, 66
Herbed Honey-Roasted Tomatoes, 230
Lemon Rosemary Chicken, 126
Salmon with 3 Spice Rubs, 106
Skirt Steak Strips with Tahini Herb Sauce,
148
HONEY
Herbed Honey-Roasted Tomatoes, 230
Honey-Glazed Sunflower Seed Chicken,
138
Honey Mustard Chicken and Steak Dinner,
144
Honey Mustard Pretzel Bites, 94
Rice Noodle Dinner, 145
Seared Sriracha Honey Salmon, 114
HUMMUS
Cucumber Roll Ups, 28
Hummus Eggplant Topper, 225

I

Ice Cream Sandwiches, 255

K

KALE
Baked Mini Falafel Ball Salad, 82
Crunchy Chicken Kale Salad, 22
Kale Chicken, 122
Kale Falafel, 83
Kale Rice Rolls, 71
Panko-Topped Kale Salad, 70
Shredded Kale and Brussels Sprouts
Salad, 74
Skirt Steak Tahini Salad, 149
Keto Cheese Crust Pizza, 182

L

Lasagna, Zoodle, 177
LEEKS
Caramelized Leek and Broccoli Soup, 54
Caramelized Leek and Cauliflower Soup, 55
LEMON
Baby Romaine Halves with Lemon
Dressing, 76
Classic Fruit Flan, 260
Lemon Dill Fish, 112
Lemon Herbed Bone Marrow, 34
Lemon Herbed Salmon Rolls with
Asparagus, 98

Lemon-Mint Mini Peppers, 220
Lemon Parfait, 261
Lemon Rosemary Chicken, 126

LENTILS
Avocado Lentil Salad, 68
Healthy Tomato Lentil Soup, 50
Lentil Cauliflower Salad, 205

LETTUCE
Baby Romaine Halves with Lemon Dressing, 76
BBQ Romaine Salad, 77
Brisket Boats, 159
Caesar Crisp Salad, 181
Rainbow Bright Salad, 80
Summery Feta Salad, 174

Lollipops, Candied Marshmallow, 278

M

MANGO
Barley Poke Bowl, 213
Cayenne-Lime Mango and Watermelon, 274
Crouton Farro Salad, 212
Hawaiian Poke Bowl, 92
Rainbow Bright Salad, 80

Maple-Glazed Japanese Sweet Potatoes, 218

MARSHMALLOWS
Candied Marshmallow Lollipops, 278
Marshmallow Cake, 279

Meatball Mushroom Sloppy Joes, 163

Meatballs with Mushrooms, 162

MINT
Fresh Orzo Salad, 210
Lemon-Mint Mini Peppers, 220
Mint Chocolate Chip Cookies, 254
Orzo Pepper Cups, 211

Muffins, Double Chocolate, 245

MUSHROOMS
Chunky Mushroom Soup, 46
Low Cal Cauliflower Mushroom Risotto, 172
Meatball Mushroom Sloppy Joes, 163
Meatballs with Mushrooms, 162
Turkey Wrapped Enoki Mushrooms, 16

N

Nachos, Tuna, 109

NOODLES
Asian Rice Salad with Wasabi Peas, 206

Rice Noodle Dinner, 145

NUTS. *SEE* ALMONDS; CASHEWS; PEANUTS; PECANS

O

OATS
Afternoon Snack Bars, 272
Endive Boat Salad, 67
Fresh Herb Granola Salad, 66
Granola Balls, 273
Granola Crusted "Breakfast" Tart, 184
High-Fiber Salad Topper, 88
Sweet Granola Chicken, 118

ONIONS
French Fried Onion Salmon, 96
Pretty Roasted Onion Flowers, 226
Roasted Onion Quinoa Salad, 208
Salmon Bagels, 97

P

PANKO
Panko-Topped Kale Salad, 70
Panko Garlic Cherry Tomatoes, 197
Toasted Garlic Panko Topping, 44

Parfait, Lemon, 261

PARSLEY
Avocado Pesto Spaghetti, 190
Endive Boat Salad, 67
Fresh Herb Granola Salad, 66
Skirt Steak Strips with Tahini Herb Sauce, 148

PARSNIPS
Feta Quinoa Hash, 193
Lazy Hash and Egg Dinner, 192
Saucy Miami Ribs with Parsnips, 156

PASTA. *SEE ALSO* NOODLES
Avocado Pesto Spaghetti, 190
Fresh Orzo Salad, 210
Orzo Pepper Cups, 211

PEACHES
Peach Crisps, 249
Summery Feta Salad, 174

Peanut Butter Chocolate Popcorn, 250

Peanut Butter Sweet Potatoes, 234

PEANUTS
Afternoon Snack Bars, 272
Asian Rice Salad with Wasabi Peas, 206
Granola Balls, 273
Peanut Butter Sweet Potatoes, 234

PEARS
Cinnamon Sugar Pears, 43
Sweet Potato Pear Soup, 42

PEAS
Pea Shoot Salad, 64
Three-Toned Cabbage Salad, 84

Pea Shoot Salad, 64

PECANS
Fresh Orzo Salad, 210
Orzo Pepper Cups, 211
Pretty Brussels Sprouts Salad, 78
Quinoa Brussels Sprouts Salad, 79

PEPPERS
Bread Cup Ideas, 33
Garlic Shishito Peppers, 216
Grilled Chicken Skewers, 133
Lemon-Mint Mini Peppers, 220
Marinated Hot Pepper Brisket, 154
Orzo Pepper Cups, 211
Pepper Dill Fish, 113
Peppers 'n Dip, 63
Rainbow Bright Salad, 80
Roasted Pepper Wraps, 221
Simply Sweet Mini Pepper Salad, 62
Sweet Potato Brisket, 155

PINEAPPLE
Hawaiian Poke Bowl, 92

PIZZA
Deli Hash Brown Pizza, 241
Keto Cheese Crust Pizza, 182

POMEGRANATE SEEDS
BBQ Romaine Salad, 77
Pretty Brussels Sprouts Salad, 78
Pretty Pomegranate Salmon, 100
Quinoa Brussels Sprouts Salad, 79

POPCORN
Peanut Butter Chocolate Popcorn, 250
Spiced Popcorn Topping, 45

POTATOES. *SEE ALSO* SWEET POTATOES
Chip-Topped Green Beans, 228
Crustless Baby Red Potato Quiche, 178
Deli Hash Brown Pizza, 241
Green Bean Salad, 229
Hash Brown "Potato Kugel" Waffles, 240
Healing Celery Soup, 40
Potato Latke Schnitzel, 142
Salted Baby Potatoes, 238

Pretzel Bites, Honey Mustard, 94

PUMPKIN SEEDS
Afternoon Snack Bars, 272
Candied Brown Rice Salad, 200
Cheesy Seed Crisps, 180
Crunch Topping, 201

Crunchy Chicken Kale Salad, 22
Crunchy Seed Topping, 44
Granola Balls, 273
High-Fiber Salad Topper, 88
Pumpkin Seed Chicken, 139
Roasted Onion Quinoa Salad, 208
Three-Toned Cabbage Salad, 84

Q

QUICHE
Cauliflower Quiche, 189
Crustless Baby Red Potato Quiche, 178

QUINOA
Cheesy Seed Crisps, 180
Feta Quinoa Hash, 193
Mediterranean Quinoa Salad, 202
Quinoa Brussels Sprouts Salad, 79
Roasted Onion Quinoa Salad, 208
Vegetarian Vegetable Quinoa Soup, 52

R

RICE
Asparagus and Rice, 223
Candied Brown Rice Salad, 200
Hawaiian Poke Bowl, 92
Jasmine Coconut and Cranberry Rice, 198
Sesame Seed Rice Balls, 18
Short Rib Chunks with Rice, 161
Taco Bowl Night, 166

RICE PAPER WRAPPERS
Deli Rice Rolls, 25
Kale Rice Rolls, 71

Risotto, Low Cal Cauliflower Mushroom, 172
Rosemary Lemon Chicken, 126

S

SALADS
Asian Rice Salad with Wasabi Peas, 206
Avocado Lentil Salad, 68
Baby Romaine Halves with Lemon Dressing, 76
Baked Mini Falafel Ball Salad, 82
Barley Poke Bowl, 213
BBQ Romaine Salad, 77
Black and White Avocado Salad, 72
Caesar Crisp Salad, 181
Candied Brown Rice Salad, 200
Crouton Farro Salad, 212

Crunchy Chicken Kale Salad, 22
Dragon Fruit Salad, 276
Endive Boat Salad, 67
Fresh Herb Granola Salad, 66
Fresh Orzo Salad, 210
Green Bean Salad, 229
Hemp Heart Cucumber Salad, 86
Kale Falafel, 83
Lentil Cauliflower Salad, 205
Mediterranean Quinoa Salad, 202
No-Mayo Avocado Tuna Salad, 108
Panko-Topped Kale Salad, 70
Pea Shoot Salad, 64
Pretty Brussels Sprouts Salad, 78
Quinoa Brussels Sprouts Salad, 79
Rainbow Bright Salad, 80
Roasted Onion Quinoa Salad, 208
Salad Bowls, 219
Salmon Salad, 103
Shredded Kale and Brussels Sprouts Salad, 74
Simply Sweet Mini Pepper Salad, 62
Skirt Steak Tahini Salad, 149
Spicy Roasted Cauliflower and Chickpea Salad, 204
Summery Feta Salad, 174
Three-Toned Cabbage Salad, 84

SALAD TOPPINGS
Crunch Topping, 201
High-Fiber Salad Topper, 88

Salami Hasselback Chicken, 128

SALMON
Fig Salmon, 101
French Fried Onion Salmon, 96
Hawaiian Poke Bowl, 92
Honey Mustard Pretzel Bites, 94
Lemon Herbed Salmon Rolls with Asparagus, 98
Pretty Pomegranate Salmon, 100
Salmon Bagels, 97
Salmon Salad, 103
Salmon with 3 Spice Rubs, 106
Seared Sriracha Honey Salmon, 114
"Smashed" Salmon, 102
Topped Sriracha Salmon, 115

SANDWICHES
Club Sandwiches, 165
Ice Cream Sandwiches, 255
Meatball Mushroom Sloppy Joes, 163
Salmon Bagels, 97

SESAME SEEDS
Black and White Avocado Salad, 72
Black Sesame–Crusted Fish, 104
Cheesy Seed Crisps, 180
Crunchy Seed Topping, 44

"Everything Bagel" Asparagus, 222
Salmon with 3 Spice Rubs, 106
Seared Sriracha Honey Salmon, 114
Sesame-Crusted London Broil, 150
Sesame Seed Rice Balls, 18
Topped Sriracha Salmon, 115

Shortcake, Coconut Strawberry, 266
Sloppy Joes, Meatball Mushroom, 163
Snack Bars, Afternoon, 272
Soup Bread Bowls, 57

SOUPS
Caramelized Leek and Broccoli Soup, 54
Caramelized Leek and Cauliflower Soup, 55
Chunky Mushroom Soup, 46
Dinner Steak Soup, 58
Healing Celery Soup, 40
Healthy Tomato Lentil Soup, 50
Roasted Kabocha Squash Soup, 56
Spiralized Noodle Soup, 48
Sweet Potato Pear Soup, 42
Tofu Soup, 59
Vegetarian Vegetable Quinoa Soup, 52
Zoodle Chicken Soup, 49

SOUP TOPPINGS
Crunchy Seed Topping, 44
Spiced Popcorn Topping, 45
Toasted Garlic Panko Topping, 44

SPINACH
Deli Egg Rolls, 24
Deli Rice Rolls, 25
Feta Quinoa Hash, 193
Lazy Hash and Egg Dinner, 192
Rainbow Bright Salad, 80

Spread, Bone Marrow, 35

SQUASH. SEE ALSO ZUCCHINI
Deli-Wrapped Squash Bites, 20
Roasted Kabocha Squash Soup, 56
Spaghetti Squash Chicken, 140
Zoodle Cheese Nests, 176
Zoodle Lasagna, 177

SRIRACHA
Seared Sriracha Honey Salmon, 114
Topped Sriracha Salmon, 115

STRAWBERRIES
Coconut Strawberry Shortcake, 266
Dragon Fruit Salad, 276
Strawberry Almond Tart, 248

SUNFLOWER SEEDS
Candied Brown Rice Salad, 200
Cheesy Seed Crisps, 180
Crunch Topping, 201
Crunchy Chicken Kale Salad, 22
Crunchy Seed Topping, 44

High-Fiber Salad Topper, 88
Honey-Glazed Sunflower Seed Chicken, 138

SWEET POTATOES
Feta Quinoa Hash, 193
Lazy Hash and Egg Dinner, 192
Maple-Glazed Japanese Sweet Potatoes, 218
Mediterranean Quinoa Salad, 202
Peanut Butter Sweet Potatoes, 234
Salad Bowls, 219
Sheet Pan Chicken with Heirloom Carrots
    and Sweet Potatoes, 120
Spiralized Noodle Soup, 48
Sweet Potato Brisket, 155
Sweet Potato Pear Soup, 42
Sweet Potato Schnitzel, 143
Vegetarian Vegetable Quinoa Soup, 52
Zoodle Chicken Soup, 49

T

Taco Bowl Night, 166

Tacos, Fish, 105

TAHINI
Fig Salmon, 101
Mediterranean Quinoa Salad, 202
Pretty Pomegranate Salmon, 100
Skirt Steak Strips with Tahini Herb Sauce,
    148

Skirt Steak Tahini Salad, 149

TARTS
Broccoli Tart, 187
Coconut Chocolate Tart, 264
Granola Crusted "Breakfast" Tart, 184
Rose Petal Apple Tart, 270
Strawberry Almond Tart, 248

Tofu Soup, 59

TOMATOES
Avocado Lentil Salad, 68
Bruschetta London Broil, 152
Cute Baguette Cups, 32
Healthy Tomato Lentil Soup, 50
Hemp Heart Cucumber Salad, 86
Herbed Honey-Roasted Tomatoes, 230
Kale Rice Rolls, 71
London Broil Crostini, 153
Panko Garlic Cherry Tomatoes, 197
Panko-Topped Kale Salad, 70
Rainbow Bright Salad, 80
Tomato Garlic Chicken, 134
Topped Sriracha Salmon, 115

TUNA
Hawaiian Poke Bowl, 92
No-Mayo Avocado Tuna Salad, 108
Tuna Nachos, 109

TURKEY
Deli Egg Rolls, 24
Deli Rice Rolls, 25

Turkey-Wrapped Enoki Mushrooms, 16

V

VEGETABLES. *SEE ALSO* **SPECIFIC
VEGETABLES**
Bread Cup Ideas, 33
Keto Cheese Crust Pizza, 182

W

Waffles, Hash Brown "Potato Kugel," 240

Wasabi Peas, Asian Rice Salad with, 206

Watermelon and Mango, Cayenne-Lime, 274

Z

Zaatar Avocado, 30

ZUCCHINI
Spiralized Noodle Soup, 48
Vegetarian Vegetable Quinoa Soup, 52
Zoodle Cheese Nests, 176
Zoodle Chicken Soup, 49
Zoodle Lasagna, 177

THANK YOU

Deena Adatto • Natalie Adelman • Sarena Alloul • Rosalie Antman • Tali Berger • Chayala Bistricer •
Melissa Blanchman • Talia Borenstein • Talia Diamond • Yael Eis • Barbara Engler • Robyn Feldberg • Shani
Finkle • Leah Fruchter • Tamar Katz • Nenita Krongold • Fraydi Kutner • Danna Galed • Naomi Glustein
• Sara Gold • Noa Goldberg • Ariella Goldstein • Leba Grauer • Daniella Greenspan • Emily Hershtal •
Natalie Hirschel • Sheri Horlick • Shoshana Iankelevic • Yael Katzman • Orah Katzman • Vivian Khul •
Pamela Khul • Nenita Krongold • Sara Lass • Resa Litwack • Ahuva Magder • CG Polirer • Abi Radcliffe
• Hailey Remer • Miri Rosen • Shoshana Schachter • Pearl Schusheim • Dina Schoiner • Amy Schwartz •
Tova Segal • Sherri Silver • Talla Silver • Donny Silver • Cheryl Stein • Yitzi Taber • Chantal Ulmer • Ariela
Vatenmakher • Avital Welsz • Becca Wertman • Joelle Yavin • Samara Yunger

To all my fantastic recipe testers — you've played such an important role in getting my recipes and
cookbook ready. Thank you so much for all the time you committed, your dedication and insightful
feedback! I so much appreciate it.

XO
Daniella